Positively Parents

CARING FOR A SEVERELY DISABLED CHILD

Bryony Beresford

SOCIAL POLICY RESEARCH UNIT

ISBN 0 11 701837 6

The Joseph Rowntree Foundation has supported this project as part of its programme of research and innovative development projects, which it hopes will be of value to policy makers and practitioners. The facts presented and views expressed in this report, however, are those of the author and not necessarily those of the Foundation.

British Library Cataloguing in Publication Data

A CIP catalogue entry for this book is available from the British Library.

Acknowledgements

First and foremost my thanks go to the families who participated in the research project on which this book is based. It was their hope that by taking part they would help families who are caring for a disabled child. It was my pleasure to talk to them and to present their views and experiences to a wider audience.

I am also grateful for the support and advice which was always available from colleagues at SPRU, during both the research project and the preparation of this book. In particular I would like to thank Dot Lawton, Julie Seymour, Michael Hirst and Patricia Thornton.

The research was funded by the Joseph Rowntree Foundation. I am grateful to the members of my Advisory Group for their advice, interest and enthusiasm throughout the project.

Contents

List of tables

Introduction

How do parents cope with the daily hassles and long-term strains of caring for a disabled child? What enables them to continue to care for their child? What keeps parents going day by day? What role does the child play in parents' ability to cope? How important are support networks for these parents? Do services help or hinder the coping process? These are some of the questions being voiced by practitioners, researchers, lay people and even parents themselves about families who are caring for and bringing up a disabled child. Drawing on the findings of an in-depth study of 20 families caring for a severely disabled child, this book will attempt to answer these questions. First, however, it is important to consider the context in which this study was undertaken, and the theoretical underpinning of the research.

Research and caring
The past 20 years have seen significant changes in thinking about the best ways to meet the needs of disabled people. In particular, there has been a shift from institutional care to care in the community. Policy reforms and lobbying from carers themselves have put the whole caring issue high on research agendas over the past decade. As a result, a considerable body of literature on caring and carers already exists and researchers are now exploring the most pertinent ways of moving forward (Parker, 1992a).

Three strands of work can be identified within research on caring. First, there is a large body of descriptive epidemiological work which has sought to establish the incidence of caring and the types of care task carried out (for example, Green, 1988; Parker and Lawton, 1994). Secondly, there exists an equally substantial literature on the experiences of being a carer (for example, Glendinning, 1983; Lewis and Meredith, 1988; Qureshi and Walker, 1989; Parker, 1992b). This has included descriptions of the stresses and burdens associated with caring for a disabled person and identifying the so-called costs (financial, emotional and physical) of care (for example, Baldwin, 1985; Quine and Pahl, 1989; Braithwaite, 1990). Thirdly, and partly in response to research findings, the needs of carers and the provision of services to meet these needs have been explored (Moore and Green, 1985; Sloper and Turner, 1992; Stallard and Lenton, 1992; Twigg and Atkin, 1993; Wishart *et al.*, 1993).

More recently, work seeking to identify factors which predispose vulnerability to stress and the aspects of caring which are particularly stressful has been pursued as a way forward for caring research (Quine and Pahl, 1985). There are however limits to such work and the findings so far have been inconclusive. Factors intuitively thought of as the cause of increased stress, such as the nature of impairment and level of dependency, have not been found to be particularly strong predictors of stress in carers (Zarit, 1989; Parker, 1992a).

A new model for carer research
The current model of carer research emphasises the often stressful and difficult nature of caring, and the adverse effects of caring on the carer. Recently an alternative model has been suggested which takes a different approach. It is seen by some as having the potential to offer new insights into caring (Byrne and Cunningham, 1985; Parker, 1992a). The basic premise of this alternative model is that it is essential, given that carers have to deal with the increased burdens and stresses of care, to find out how carers *cope* with these stresses, and what factors help them to cope. This approach redefines the issue of caring in a number of ways. First, it does not pathologise caring, that is, it does not assume that caring invariably has an adverse effect on the carer. Secondly, the fact that many carers do adapt and cope with their situation is emphasised. Thirdly, carers are redefined as active agents as opposed to passive recipients of an onslaught of carer-related stress. What carers actually do to manage problems and difficulties becomes the focus of attention. This shift in approach can be attributed to developments both within academic disciplines where research on caring has taken place, and to the ways in which the notions of social and personal welfare are being reconceptualised within social policy.

In recent years, psychological and, to a lesser extent, sociological research on families caring for a disabled member has increasingly tended to adopt a 'stress and coping' approach. This has been informed by highly developed theoretical models of stress, coping and well-being which, although essentially psychological, have also been adopted by sociologists. The findings from research using this approach are promising. Both the ways individuals cope with stress and a number of personal and social factors have been shown to be more predictive of carers' well-being than the more traditional predictors such as severity of disability and care needs (Quine and Pahl, 1991; Sloper et al., 1991; Sloper and Turner, 1993). However, it is only recently that social policy has begun to draw on this work both in terms of setting research agendas and informing policy and practice (see, for example, Titterton, 1992; Milne et al., 1993).

Within social policy the traditional approach to welfare research, that is research on individuals whose well-being is threatened by adverse events or difficult circumstances, has been criticised by a number of commentators on several counts (Fennell *et al.*, 1988; Titterton, 1992). First, it is seen as pathologising individuals into homogeneous problem groups, such as 'the elderly', 'the disabled', 'the unemployed'. Secondly, individuals are conceived as 'passive recipients of welfare services' (Titterton, 1992, p.1). Thirdly, no account is taken of the ways individuals actively seek to respond to and resolve events impinging on their lives.

In his seminal paper on welfare research Michael Titterton (1992) argued:

> ...a new approach to the study of welfare is called for, one which is sensitive to the heterogeneous nature of vulnerability and risk, and which can account for the creative problem-solving of diverse individuals in the face of adversity.
> (p.5)

In searching for a literature to inform debate on this new model of welfare, Titterton saw the work on life events, stress and coping as particularly relevant. Indeed he specifically drew on that model of stress and coping most favoured by research into caring being carried out by psychologists and sociologists, to which we have already referred.

The research approach
We report here on a study which adopted a new approach to carer research. This book therefore takes a different stance from much of the work on families with disabled children. Instead of focusing on the negative aspects of caring for a disabled child, the project recognised the importance of looking at how parents cope with the difficulties they face. We cast parents in a new role in which they are seen as actively managing their situation.

Taking such an approach is important. All too often research has gone no further than describing the problems parents face (for example, Tizard and Grad, 1961; Hewett, 1970; Chetwynd, 1985). Some work has focused on the role of services in ameliorating these problems (for example, Burden, 1980; Jefford, 1990; Bose, 1991). Few writers have included in their accounts what the parents them-selves do. Without this, our understanding of the lives of families caring for a disabled child will remain incomplete. Our study is a contribution to increasing this understanding, and we hope that our findings will be used by service providers, policy makers, researchers and parents.

A lot of the adult books are really depressing. They really go to town on the difficulty with it. That is an important side of it, the down side. But you've got to be left with some hope. (Walker, parent of a child with autism)

Fundamental principles – resources and strategies

The approach adopted by this project was informed by a theoretical model known as the process model of stress and coping (Lazarus and Folkman, 1984). The premise of this model is that the coping process mediates the impact of stress on an individual's well-being. The two key aspects of the coping process are coping resources and coping strategies.

In order to understand how parents manage to care for their disabled child it must be remembered that a number of factors will influence how a parent handles a particular difficulty. These factors determine whether the parent regards an event or situation as stressful, and also what the parent will do to solve or relieve the stress. Such factors are known as *resources*. There are social and personal resources. Social resources include money, practical resources and the availability of support from individuals and services. Personal factors include a parent's beliefs, approach to life, mental and physical health, skills and aspects of personality. Where resources are few or over-stretched, the individual becomes more vulnerable to stress and its adverse effects.

Although something is known about the resources parents use, we know little about what parents actually *do* when they encounter the practical and emotional stresses associated with caring for a disabled child. The actions and thoughts used to deal with stress are known as *strategies*. The strategies available to a parent are mediated by the parent's resources. For example, a parent cannot deal with emotional distress by talking to a friend if no such friend exists. Similarly, a parent cannot ease the burden of housework by paying for a cleaner unless there is money available to do so.

Strategies have a number of functions. Not all the stresses parents face as they care for and bring up their child can be solved or overcome. Sometimes parents have to learn ways of dealing with the fact that a particular problem will always be present in their lives. In this instance the goal therefore is not to solve the problem but to handle it in such a way that it has as little impact on the parent as possible. Thus strategies include efforts both to *master* and to *manage* stress. Sometimes an individual simply does not have the appropriate resources to master a stressor. In the context of this research project, the extent to which health, education and social services are adequate resources for parents is an important consideration.

Organisation of the book

This book is based on a study of 20 families caring for a severely disabled child. The following chapter outlines the methodology used and describes the sample. Chapters Three and Four focus on the ways parents used informal and formal support, and Chapter Five explores the function of financial and practical, or utilitarian resources. In Chapters Six and Seven the role of the child and the parent-child relationship in the coping process is examined. The strategies parents used are described in Chapter Eight. A longitudinal perspective to the research is provided in Chapter Nine, where the effects of changes in parents' circumstances over the research period are examined. The final chapter discusses the implications of the study's findings in terms of policy and practice relating to families caring for a disabled child.

The parents and their children

This chapter briefly describes the research process. We explain the reasoning behind setting up certain 'inclusion' criteria for the families involved in the research. The way families were selected and recruited is described. The second half of the chapter serves to provide the reader with an overview of the parents (and their children) who took part in this study. Finally, the scene is set for the rest of the book as we describe the types of stresses that these parents faced as they cared for their disabled child.

Choosing the families

The focus of the study was on how parents managed the long-term situation of caring for a disabled child. Twenty parents caring for a severely disabled child were interviewed in depth on two occasions. The principal aim of the interviews was to discover the resources and strategies used by parents as they coped with the care of their child. On the first occasion the interviewer sought to discover as much as possible about the daily lives of these families which might be relevant to understanding how they cope. Second interviews were conducted around four to five months after the first interview. Only one parent was unwilling to be revisited. The second interview explored the impact of any changes in the family's circumstances and also afforded the opportunity to pursue issues raised at the first interview.

In order that other issues relating to families with disabled children did not intrude on our research question, we imposed certain inclusion criteria on the sample selected. These were:

- a definite diagnosis of the child's condition had been made

- at least one year had elapsed since the diagnosis

- the condition was not immediately life-threatening

- the parent was the natural/biological parent of the child

- the child was aged between 18 months and 12 years

- no other members of the household required extra care.

We decided that it was important for families included in the study to have some form of diagnosis for their child's disability. With a diagnosis usually comes some knowledge about the reasons for the disability, the possible outcomes and prognosis. Parents usually feel that having a diagnosis, whatever it is, is infinitely preferable to not knowing what is wrong with the child (Brown and Hepple, 1989). We wanted to exclude from the study families who were, in a sense, still searching for a diagnosis, because their needs and concerns were likely to be different. At the same time, however, some children never receive a 'medical' diagnosis, especially where the child has learning difficulties. In these instances the only diagnosis may be 'severe developmental delay'. We did include families who had been given such a 'diagnosis', and whose child had been discharged from hospital care with no further investigations pending.

Although we have argued that having a diagnosis is preferable to parents, there is still a period of time after the birth of a disabled child or the onset of a disability when the family goes through a process of adaptation. During this period parents not only have to deal with the care needs of the child, but also come to terms with their emotional reactions. This period has been well researched, and the evidence suggests that it can take over a year for families to settle into a pattern of adaptation (Gath, 1985; Leventhal *et al.*, 1985; Farran *et al.*, 1986). Since this project was focusing on coping with the long-term stresses and strains of care, only families where the diagnosis had been made at least one year previously were included.

The stresses associated with caring for a child who is soon likely to die are also very different. For this reason, and also because it seemed highly insensitive to intrude on families at that time, we excluded families where the child's condition was immediately life-threatening.

Intuitively it would seem that the experiences of fostering a child with disabilities can be very different to those of natural or biological parents. For example, the emotional burden may well differ. In addition, foster parents receive greater financial help than natural parents. Because of these differences, we chose to exclude foster families.

All parents face daily demands associated with bringing up and caring for a child. Many of these activities fit the definition of caring; that is, a supportive activity, usually taking place within family structures, in which the carer has responsibility for the cared-for person and there is some degree of emotional involvement (Twigg and Atkin, 1993). It could therefore be argued that all parents are carers. However, when the child is healthy, such tasks are known as parenting (Crnic and Booth, 1991) as opposed to caring. The qualitative differences between parenting and caring seem to hinge on notions of 'going beyond what is normal' (Moroney, 1976; Cameron and Sturge-Moore, 1990)). Clearly linked to this is the child's age. Many parenting tasks become caring tasks when they are carried out for a child over a certain age (Glendinning, 1983). It has been argued therefore that since, in most cases, the needs of a young baby, whether or not disabled, are very much the same, the distinction between caring and parenting is unclear. For this reason, families whose disabled child was less than eighteen months were excluded from the study. We also decided to impose an upper age limit. When any child reaches adolescence new issues relating to independence, puberty, secondary schooling and leaving school emerge (Richardson and Ritchie, 1986; Wikler, 1986; Quine and Pahl, 1989). We did not feel that these issues fell within the boundaries we had defined for the project. As a result, an upper age limit of 12 years was used.

The final inclusion criteria was that no other member of the household required 'extra' care, apart from child care of healthy siblings. There has been much research to suggest that care of frail, elderly or disabled people can be an enormous burden for families (for example, Levin et al., 1989; Gilleard et al., 1984; Braithwaite, 1990). To include families who had a double burden of care would, we felt, be inappropriate and distract from the purpose of the study.

The sample was drawn from families who had successfully applied to the Family Fund. The Family Fund gives modest grants to families who are on a moderate to low income and are caring for a very severely disabled child. At the time of the study the Fund was receiving about eight hundred new applications each month, and therefore constituted a unique and large sampling frame.

Given the very specific list of inclusion criteria, a rigorous process of screening and selection was used. The screening process was incorporated into normal Family Fund application procedures and Family Fund Visiting Social Workers were asked to collect the necessary screening information during their assessment visits to 700 families. This technique was used in preference to a postal survey which, it was felt, would be biased against parents with language or literacy difficulties. Screening data were collected from 640 families. This was used to select families who fulfilled the inclusion criteria and who also represented a range of living circumstances and parental stress. Parents were recruited by a letter inviting them to take part in the study. Of those approached, just under 60 per cent of parents agreed to take part. The interviews were tape-recorded and later transcribed. These verbatim transcripts were analysed in order to abstract information about the coping processes of families caring for a severely disabled child.

The parents

The parents were geographically dispersed throughout England and Wales. Table 1 summarises the key demographic features of the sample. Names have been changed to preserve anonymity.

Table 1:   Characteristics of parents

Name	Living circumstances	Level of stress	Lone parent	Rural or urban	No. of children in household
ABBOTT	Poor	High	–	Urban	1
BARON[1]	Poor	Low	–	Urban	3
CARVER	Poor	Low	Yes	Urban	3
CURREY	Poor	High	Yes	Urban	2
DAVIES	Good	Low	–	Urban	2
DOBSON	Good	Low	–	Urban	2
FORSYTH	Good	High	–	Urban	2
GREENHOW	Good	Low	–	Urban	2
HODDER	Good	Low	–	Urban	2
LOFT	Good	Low	–	Rural	2
MAHMOOD[2]	Poor	High	Yes	Urban	1
NICHOLSON	Good	High	–	Urban	1
OHRI[3]	Poor	–[4]	–	Urban	1
REEVES	Good	High	–	Urban	2
THOMPSON[5]	Poor	Low	Yes	Rural	1
VYNER	Poor	Low	Yes	Rural	1
WALKER	Good	High	–	Urban	3
WHITING	Good	High	–	Rural	2
WHITTON	Poor	High	–	Urban	3
WILLIAMS	Poor	High	Yes	Rural	2

Notes on table:
[1] This parent was a traveller/gypsy
[2] This parent was Pakistani
[3] This parent was Bengali
[4] At the time of the interview it emerged that the father had completed this measure and not the mother
[5] This parent was the child's father

All held main responsibility for the care of the child, and all but one were mothers, reflecting current patterns of child care in Britain (Bridgwood and Savage, 1993). Six were lone parents including the only father in the study. Five parents lived in a rural location, with the remainder living in towns or cities. Ten families were assessed as having good living circumstances, and the other ten as having poor living circumstances. Half the sample reported a high number of stress symptoms and nine parents were assessed as having few stress symptoms. The stress symptom score for the tenth parent was rendered invalid because the father had completed the stress questionnaire and not the mother. The data were based on scores from a single measure of stress and should only be used as indicator of stress levels among our sample. In six households the disabled child was the only child. Included in this figure is one family where there were two adult siblings who no longer lived at home. Ten parents had two children and the remaining four households had three children. Finally, three parents belonged to minority groups. One parent was Pakistani, another was from Bangladesh and the third was a gypsy or traveller who, at the time of the study, was living in a semi-permanent site created by the local council.

The children

Table 2 provides a summary of the key characteristics of the children.

Table 2: Key characteristics of children

Child's name	Age (years)	Gender	Diagnosis	Impairment
Angela ABBOTT	2	Girl	Developmental delay	Learning
Patrick BARON	3	Boy	No muscles in arms or shoulders	Physical
John CARVER	5	Boy	Developmental delay	Learning
Ian CURREY	2	Boy	Cerebral palsy	Physical**
Debbie DAVIES	4½	Girl	Juvenile Chronic Poly-Arthritis	Physical
Anna DOBSON	6½	Girl	Severe learning difficulties	Learning
Mark FORSYTH	6½	Boy	Asperger syndrome*	Social
Alan GREENHOW	10	Boy	Duchenne muscular dystrophy	Physical
Jenny HODDER	8	Girl	Cerebral palsy	Physical**
Martin LOFT	7	Boy	Perthes disease	Physical
Safraz MAHMOOD	4	Boy	Developmental delay	Learning
Caroline NICHOLSON	3½	Girl	Cerebral palsy	Physical**
Shamit OHRI	5	Boy	Leukaemia	Physical
Lisa REEVES	5	Girl	Cerebral palsy	Physical**
Louise THOMPSON	5	Girl	Optic Hydroplasia (blindness)	Physical
Ben VYNER	7	Boy	Albinism	Physical
Richard WALKER	5	Boy	Asperger syndrome*	Social
Amanda WHITING	2½	Girl	Down's syndrome	Learning
Paul WHITTON	8	Boy	Down's syndrome	Learning
David WILLIAMS	3	Boy	Cerebral palsy	Physical**

Notes on table:
* Asperger syndrome is a form of autism where there is high (intellectual) functioning.
** It is often difficult to ascertain the degree of mental impairment in children with cerebral palsy due to the severity of physical impairment.

The children were aged between two and ten years. Twelve were boys and eight were girls. In all but five cases a diagnosis had been made. Where there was no specific diagnosis, four children had been described as being developmentally delayed and the fifth child had no muscles in his arms or shoulders. In terms of the nature of the disability, for seven children the impairment was physical, six children had learning difficulties, five had complex disabilities and two children had severe social and communication problems. There were differences in the prognosis of the various conditions represented within this group, though the majority were chronic, lifelong conditions. In contrast, one child had Perthes disease which is a transitory orthopaedic condition in which recovery is expected within five years. In addition, for the child with no muscles in his arms or shoulders and the child with juvenile chronic poly-arthritis there was the possibility that certain treatments might significantly improve their conditions, though this was by no means definite.

The stresses of caring for a disabled child

It is important to set the context of our investigation by describing the range of stresses which parents encountered. Most of the parents in our study found that the stresses associated with the care and bringing up of their disabled child were wide-ranging, unrelenting and sometimes overwhelming.

However, parents did not always perceive their disabled child as the major source of stress in their lives. Instead, other difficulties, such as marital problems, poverty and bereavement, presented far greater problems or distress.

> I think finding the money to survive is the most difficult thing. Trying to keep everything together and not take it out on the children when it's all falling apart like when a big bill comes in. That is the most difficult, I don't see David [disabled child] as a problem at all. I never have seen him as a problem.
> (Williams)

Other parents felt the stresses they experienced were more associated with the pressures of bringing up a family rather than specifically resulting from having a disabled child.

> The fact that I've got two young children is probably harder to cope with than the fact that Amanda's got Downs [syndrome].
> (Whiting)

Finally, one or two parents did not feel that their child presented them with any particular difficulties.

> Sometimes I think he [disabled child] isn't any more of a handful than the other two [children]. I can't say I worry about

him any more than the rest. I worry about his development, yes. But I don't worry about him in any other ways because he's just the same as having the others.
(Carver)

It could be argued that all these parents were no longer conscious of the stresses and problems caused by their child. The passage of time meant that such difficulties had become integrated into what to them was 'normal' family life. Alternatively, it might be that, since some of the children in our study were quite young, parents had not experienced certain difficulties, or that the extent to which the needs of the child differed from a non-disabled child of a similar age had not emerged. To parents of older children, what was draining was the way problems continued beyond what would be normally expected. This parent's disabled child was six and a half years old.

But it's just the having it for so many years. That's the thing. Whereas with Robert [sibling] you know as he gets older things will ease off. It's because it goes on for so long. Like we've had problems at meal times for so many years, she still won't have new shoes and you know every time you go to the shoe shop she's going to throw a tantrum.
(Dobson)

Stresses directly associated with the disabled child included meeting the child's physical or medical needs, supervising or watching over the child and dealing with sleep and behaviour problems. Furthermore, there were emotional stresses such as seeing the child in pain, or suffering from a life-threatening condition. Equally critical were stresses which, though not directly caused by the child, were associated with having a disabled child. These arose mainly from encounters with professionals and dissatisfaction with service provision. Many parents had, at one time or another, been involved in some sort of confrontation with health, education or social services. In addition, some parents had experienced adverse reactions to their child from family or members of the public. Finally, the child's disability sometimes caused other hardships. Two parents felt that the disability had been one of the factors causing the break-up of their marriage. Another problem was financial difficulties brought on by the additional costs of caring for a disabled child.

Summary

In this chapter we have reported the research process, including our reasoning behind the nature of the sample selected for the study and the way parents were recruited to the study. Key characteristics of the parents and children have been described. Finally, the scene has been set for the rest of the book. The types of stresses which parents in the study experienced as they cared for their child have been described. These included both emotional distress and practical problems and difficulties. A number of sources of stress were identified including the child's care needs, services and professionals, other people's attitudes and the effect of the disability on family circumstances.

Use of informal social support

Humans are sociable beings and derive personal strength from the relationships they have with others. The support provided by a relationship includes emotional support, information and practical help. These relationships range along a continuum from the intimacy shared between a wife and husband, to the more formal relationship between a parent and her child's doctor, for example. The type of support needs met by different kinds of relationship will vary. It is usual to make the distinction between social support which comes from informal sources and formal social support, which is provided as a service. Here we examine the use of informal social support. First, we briefly describe the sources of informal social support before looking at the types of support provided, and the factors and barriers which affect use of informal support.

Sources of informal social support

Thirteen parents were married or living as married and therefore had access to *spouse or partner support*. It should not be assumed, however, that the single parents were more vulnerable to stress because they lacked this source of support. Some lone parents had recently left relationships which had been an enormous source of stress. For them it was a relief to be alone. Perhaps the critical issue here is whether, if there is a partner, the parent feels supported. Only one parent felt unsupported by her partner and this lack of support was an additional strain in itself.

> M[1] Several times you feel you're going to snap but you carry on. You learn to keep calm, just in general.
>
> I   What would have happened if you'd snapped?
>
> M   I don't think Colin and I would be together now because that was most of the pressure, him not helping. Now I try and ignore the fact and carry on.
> (Nicholson)

Fourteen parents had other children, most of whom were less than 12 years old. Even among those with quite young children, parents

---

[1] The convention used in attributing discussion is:
I   interviewer
M   mother
F   father
S   sibling

found that the child's *siblings* provided help or support to the parent. However, the extent and nature of this support was greater where the other children were teenagers or older. In these families the parent often talked about support from the whole family, as opposed from just the spouse.

On the whole it was the grandparents who were the source of support from within *the extended family*. Previous research has shown that parents have different expectations as to the extent to which grandparents, compared to other relatives or friends, become involved in the care of children (Moss, Bolland and Foxman, 1983; Willmott, 1986). Parents feel it is more 'legitimate' to turn to grandparents for help. Indeed, it is likely that grandparents want to support the parents and are more closely attached to the child than more distant relatives. One parent, who had recently lost her mother, described the difference between turning to her own mother for support and asking her aunt for help.

> I do miss my Mum because she didn't mind having her [disabled child], because they were *the* grandchildren so to speak. Whereas, although the Aunts are very good, I don't like to impose too much really.
> (Dobson)

At the time of the study, all parents had at least one parent or parent-in-law alive. However, two parents received no support at all from the child's grandparents.

Most parents had maintained *friendships* with people they had known prior to the birth of the disabled child. Only one parent reported losing her friends as a result of telling them of her child's diagnosis. For other parents, moving to a new area because of the break-up of their marriage or, in a more extreme case, emigration, meant that they had lost touch with old friends.

There were only four parents who essentially had no contact with *other parents* who also had a child with the same condition or some other disability. Parents met other parents through a number of sources. One of the most common ways was through membership of a local parents' support group. Support groups can be regarded as falling half way between informal and formal support. Their very name indicates their function as being a legitimate arena through which support can be sought. The reason we chose to include support groups within this chapter on informal support is because it was apparent that the support parents gained through member-ship of such a group came from other members of the group, as opposed to the professionals who might be involved in running the group. Indeed, these professionals were often seen as inhibiting the support such a group could provide.

I'm giving the meetings around here time for us to get relaxed with each other and then we'll do away with the social worker. We'll become friends then, rather than a group.
(Thompson)

I know they're really trying to be helpful, but it doesn't feel like it because their ideas and my ideas are completely different. The last meeting I attended it was like 'Now we must sit here, and we must talk for five minutes about this, and we must go into different things and we must stop after...'. You can't do that if you're on a tack or something you want to follow through. It's just the way they try to organise you as if you were children at school or something.
(Carver)

Eight parents belonged to a local support group and attended their group regularly, though the frequency of meetings varied from weekly meetings to once every two months. However, only one parent mentioned having social contact with members of the group between meetings.

A few parents had met other parents through special needs play-groups. Parents using this sort of facility spoke of the benefits they experienced from taking their child along.

M And then we go for a coffee, the other parents, six of us and we all have a good talk and laugh....
I ...is that talking about your children?
M Yes...children, shopping, husbands, how they're cop-ing...but it is, it's a nice place, it's a great set up.
(Abbott)

Where the child was at school, meeting other parents was not so easy. A child in a mainstream school was usually the only disabled child at that school. Those children attending special school tended to be taken there by the school transport service, so that contact with other parents happened only on rare social occasions.

I When do you get to meet them [other parents] if Anna gets taken by bus?
M ..say when there's been open meetings or meetings at the school and you sort of give them a little wave...and gradu-ally know each other by sight. Then it was the Christmas disco, we happened to be sitting at the next table, and I said 'You'll have to come round', and it started from there.
(Dobson)

The other ways parents had met other parents was through 'friends of friends', people at work and through taking the child to hydro-therapy sessions at the local hospital.

A few parents received help or support from a *neighbour*. Most studies have shown a low involvement by neighbours in helping parents care for a disabled child (Wilkin, 1979; Glendinning, 1983; Pahl and Quine, 1985). It is important to consider why parents might not receive much support from neighbours. Perhaps the most relevant point is that five parents had family members living either as neighbours or close by. Three of these parents did not use the support of other neighbours. A further two parents lived in relatively isolated situations where there literally was not a neighbour living next door.

Practical support

Practical support could take the form of general child care, special care tasks, household duties and childminding, as well as meeting information needs.

General child care

It was not surprising to find that partners were the greatest source of support for general child care such as watching over and playing with the child and getting up in the night. Indeed when the partner was at home, it seemed that responsibility for the child often fell equally, or that the partner took over.

> He gets up at night and if he's here in the evening he'll sometimes make the tea so it's – it is more or less split down the middle when he's here.
> (Walker)

Some partners had particular responsibilities in relation to the care of the child which were of practical support. For instance, if an older child needed lifting the partner would always do that if he was in the house. It was also common to find that partners were responsible for disciplining the child or keeping control. In some cases, where the child had to be restrained, this was purely because the partner was stronger. However, it also appeared that the child responded better to the father's discipline, or would be less likely to 'play up' with the father.

> Then you get a full scale tantrum, and my husband tends to....As I say, if we were going out.. he can, whether it's just that he's just physically stronger, he can sort of pin her down.
> (Dobson)

Siblings played a small role in how parents were able to manage looking after the disabled child. For instance, having a sibling to play with kept the child occupied, and encouraged learning. This was found especially in families where the children were both quite young, and substantial differences in intellectual ability had not emerged. With regard to providing practical help to the parent, none of the siblings were reported to be carrying out any tasks that could be described as extraordinary for a child of that age. Rather they did what any child would want to do to help a brother or sister who was not fully able-bodied or who was unwell.

> She's [sibling] very helpful. If he [disabled child] drops something on the floor she'll pick it up for him and get things for him. If he goes upstairs she'll go and sit with him. In the mornings he sometimes wakes early, she'll go through and she sits with him, keeps him company.
> (Greenhow)

Special care tasks
It was extremely rare to find anyone but the main carer of the child carrying out special care tasks. There was one instance where the parent lived next door to a nurse who carried out certain procedures that the mother did not feel confident to do herself, such as giving the child a suppository. In two-parent families the partner would often support the parent as she carried out a special care task. In one family, for example, while the mother fed the child her partner prepared the evening meal so that as soon as feeding was over the mother could sit down to her own meal.

Household duties
A few parents were supported in carrying out household duties by either their partners or grandparents. However, it was unusual to find partners playing a significant role here, though there were instances of the partner supporting the parent as she carried out these tasks. Usually this involved looking after the child in some way. This parent found taking her child shopping very difficult.

> What we've been doing lately is, on a Saturday morning, my husband takes Paul to the cafe down the road and he has breakfast with him. So I often go down to Sainsburys in the van, pick them up and come home – so he's not with me.
> (Whitton)

Only the parents of children with complex disabilities received help with household tasks from grandparents. In some cases this help was considerable. In one family, the maternal grandparents visited weekly to do the housework, ironing and gardening. In another family, both sets of grandparents each cooked the family's main meal one day every week. We came across only one instance where friends helped with household duties. This was a rather exceptional case where the family belonged to an extremely supportive church.

Childminding and having a break
Clearly one of the greatest advantages for parents with partners is that they have someone with whom they are happy to leave the

child. This made it considerably easier for parents to have breaks from caring for the child. For single parents, unless other family members live nearby, finding a childminder was often difficult. In contrast, all but one parent who had a partner spoke about being able to go out in the evenings if they wanted to.

One of the greatest problems for many parents was tiredness, and partners were able to help the parents recover to some extent. It was interesting that several parents reported a similar Saturday morning routine. It is difficult to imagine how other sources of informal support could regularly substitute this sort of support.

> So Phil will say if I've had a bad week 'You stay in bed. I'll take the kids downstairs', and then I will – I might only have an hour, but that hour seems like a week.
> (Whiting)

In the two families where the siblings were considerably older than the child, they were able to help with occupying the child and childminding. As a result both families were virtually self-sufficient when it came to childminding.

> Well we go out, me and my husband go out. Susan [sibling] looks after Paul [disabled child] and we go out. We went out last night, we went out about eight o'clock 'til about ten o'clock. She's really good like that if we ever wanted to go to like a wedding or something like that...
> (Whitton)

Generally, childminding duties taken on by the extended family were for prearranged events such as work and going out. More spontaneous instances of childminding by the extended family (such as when the parent just felt at the end of her tether) were rare and depended both on the grandparents living nearby and having no other commitments. However, where such arrangements were possible, it was an enormous help to the parent.

> I   How do you get over feeling very tired?
> M   I just lie here and I say 'I'm not looking after him [disabled child] today', and my dad takes him home or my sister, she'll look after him for a while until I get a sleep.
> (Mahmood)

It was interesting to find that in virtually all cases the child was taken to the grandparents' house to be looked after. Where the grandparents lived even a moderate distance away limited, to some extent, what the parents did during their break and the frequency with which they used grandparents for child care.

> It tends to be my mother who'll have them, where she lives in B_____. So it's a matter of driving down there, leaving them

there, coming back or having a night out in B_____. But she hasn't got room for us all to stay. So it's such a lot of work to arrange a night out at the moment, so we tend not to bother. (Whiting)

Three parents found that their child's grandparents offered to help the family by having the non-disabled sibling to stay but would not have the disabled child. Sometimes this was because the grandparents could not manage the disabled child. However, parents found this exclusion of the disabled child upsetting.

Nobody offers to have Lisa. This is the type of problem we're having with the grandparents now. It's 'Can we take Kerry [sibling] so you've got some time with Lisa', but nobody ever really wants to take Lisa [disabled child]. (Reeves)

It was very rare to find friends offering or providing any form of practical support, but where it did occur it was in the form of childminding. Aside from the mother who received considerable support from her friends at church, only three other parents had used their friends as childminders. In these cases, they had only done so once or twice. In addition, where friends had looked after the disabled child, the child was either very young or was unlikely to require much care.

Finally, we came across one instance where a neighbour had offered to childmind if the parent ever needed to go out for half an hour or so. The parent found this arrangement extremely helpful since it was very difficult to 'pop out' with a child in a wheelchair.

Information
Parents of other disabled children, met either informally or through a support group, were clearly a crucial source of information about benefits, respite care facilities, schooling, treatment and practical tips.

I didn't know that we'd even be eligible for respite care until the support group, and I realised that several of the other mums have got it. (Forsyth)

Contact through a support group with parents whose disabled children were older was seen by parents as particularly beneficial. They were an important source of information about how they had overcome difficulties and could advise parents on how to pre-empt certain problems.

It's really making a difference. I'm sort of meeting mums with older children than Lisa who are able to give advice, whereas before I've only been in contact with mums with children of the same age, so they haven't gone through any different things to what you have. Whereas now, with meeting these older mums, they're able to give advice as to where they think they've gone wrong, and hopefully we can sort it out from that.
(Reeves)

Emotional support

The two most significant sources of emotional support for parents were their partners and other parents with a disabled child. However, the actual nature of the emotional support provided by these two groups of people differed considerably.

All but one of the mothers reported their partner to be a source of emotional support and strength. In many ways this support can be seen as the product of what is likely to be the most intimate relationship in a person's life. First, the fact that the partner is living in the household and is with the parent for a considerable part of the day, facilitates the extent to which the partner can help with child care and provide emotional support.

It's having somebody there who's in the some position as me. It's different for grandparents and aunties and uncles and friends than it is for us. We've got her twenty-four hours a day. It's just having somebody there who feels the same way as I do, that's there to support me.
(Whiting)

Secondly, the nature of the relationship introduces other unique factors. Most fundamental is the fact that the child is *theirs*, and that the couple have a commitment to the child. Also, the parents have a commitment to each other which no other relationship can match or imitate. Intimate knowledge of what makes the other 'tick' enables a partner to know which is the best way of supporting the parent.

Perhaps the most important way that partners provided support was that mothers knew they would be working together in caring for and bringing up their child.

We've always talked about how Mark is, what he's doing, this sort of thing, and it's always been very much a joint thing. We've both said 'Yes, there are problems and we want something doing', and we've both talked about it and we're both very involved in Mark and his care and his future.
(Forsyth)

Some couples acted as a team in mounting what were essentially campaigns to ensure that their child received the best of service provision. In these situations, not only was the partner providing practical support, in terms of collecting information, writing letters or making telephone calls, he was also supporting the mother in taking action in the first place.

    I   ..and does he [husband] support you in your decision to appeal [about child's statement]?

    M   Oh yes, totally. I wouldn't do it if he didn't. I need him behind me otherwise I don't think I would be strong enough to do it.

    (Reeves)

In addition to the support that partners could give in relation to particular difficulties, mothers also valued being able to share daily events and worries, and make decisions together.

    M   Obviously the little day-to-day things we talk about you know, little problems but..

    I   What do you mean by little problems, the day-to-day?

    F   Basically things like wanting to get social services out...

    M   ...anything, when any sort of little worries crop up we talk about it, like the extension

    F   ...or do we think Alan needs new cushions for his wheelchair.

    (Greenhow)

Partners were also privy to worries that the mother did not feel she could share with anyone else.

    I didn't say anything to my friends. It was just between me and Graham [husband], and no one really knew what I was carrying on about.

    (Dobson)

The emotional support provided by other parents of disabled children was qualitatively different from the emotional support provided by a partner. This might reflect what is known more generally about the role of close friendships, even among married women (Holter *et al.*, 1982). Indeed having another parent in whom to confide would relieve the partner from being the sole source of emotional support to the parent. Other parents of disabled children played a vital role in reducing parents' feelings of isolation. The sense of support from other parents centred around feeling understood because of shared experiences.

    We find it better to speak to someone who does know because they know, they're going through the same thing.

    (Davies)

It was enormously reassuring for a parent to find that other parents had the same worries and experienced the same difficulties with their children.

> But I find that if Amanda's [disabled child] having any particular problems that the chance to talk to somebody else about it, whose child may have experienced those problems. I mean the first thing I found really strange about Amanda was her double jointedness. I found that really hard to understand at first. But I thought it was strange so I would speak to some of the mums there, and one mum's got a little Down's syndrome boy who is about eight and she would say to me 'Oh David's exactly the same', and it would put your mind at rest.
> (Whiting)

Because they know that other parents are going through the same difficulties, parents felt able to talk to each other without being misunderstood.

> It seems as though when we get together we all have a moan and a groan, you don't ... but I think you all understand ... you know. Like we're going on holiday on Saturday and they're saying 'Oh, have a nice time – ha, ha!' and that little 'ha, ha!' – we know exactly what you mean whereas no one else would. Like my friend, she popped round today and she said 'Have a nice time' and you know she genuinely mean it, but she doesn't look beyond it and why should she? Whereas with the others, they can give a sort of 'ha, ha!' at the end and you know exactly what they mean.
> (Dobson)

This illustrates very clearly the difference between the emotional support that can be provided by a friend and that offered by other parents of disabled children. One parent who only recently had joined a support group, and had never met other parents before, was clearly thrilled.

> It's been brilliant. It's nice having other parents that have children with special needs.
> (Carver)

Finally, where parents had contact with other parents, it was clear that it was easier to turn to them for emotional support than to their other friends. The feeling of being a burden or 'moaner', which was sometimes felt when a parent was talking to a friend, was not experienced when talking to another parent. Whether at a support group meeting or just getting together informally with another parent, parents valued the opportunity to 'let off steam', 'feel depressed', 'have a moan' without feeling guilty about burdening others or 'going on'.

It was rare to find parents using other sources of informal emotional support to any great extent. If it occurred with members of the extended family, it was usually the parent's own brothers and sisters who were sources of support. In one situation the child's aunt helped the mother with fund-raising, whilst the child's uncle had helped with their applications to social services. Other parents had found it easier to discuss difficulties with aunts and uncles rather than with grandparents. In one instance, this had been made easier by the fact that the couple were also having problems:

> Phil's [husband] brother is very good. He's very supportive and helpful, and his wife. They've been closer to us since we've had Amanda [disabled child] than they were previously, but then they've had problems of their own. Although it's problems of a totally different nature we've found it easy to talk to each other, because we've both got problems.
> (Whiting)

Six parents confided in one or two of their friends and found them a source of emotional support. However, it seemed that the parents did not talk about their child to all their friends. If available, the support offered by other parents of disabled children was found to be qualitatively better.

> I mean I've got friends and that but I suppose the people that really understand are the other mums.
> (Dobson)

There was one exception to the level of emotional support provided by friends. One mother had received enormous emotional support from members of her church, both from individuals within the church and as a more collective entity. Someone had come to pray for the child every week, and had been doing so for four years. In addition the mother knew that she could turn to a twenty-four hour 'prayer chain' in a crisis. The constancy of the support and the knowledge that support was being given at some cost was, in itself, a real support to this parent.

> Well it's support in the sense that we know people care enough. I mean, if somebody comes round every week for four years you know they care. You just don't feel that you're struggling alone. You feel that all those people actually care enough to do something. It's not just words. They're actually doing something because they really care and that just lifts that feeling of struggling alone right off you.
> (Hodder)

Very occasionally neighbours were a source of emotional support. One parent found discussing her child with a neighbour served to put her child in perspective. One of the main difficulties this parent faced was taking the child shopping. She recalled what her neighbour had said when she was talking to her about this.

The woman next door, she doesn't like taking her little boy shopping because he drives her mad. She says 'Well, it's not just Paul [disabled child], you know, my kid's the same, and he's normal'.
(Whitton)

Factors affecting the type and availability of support

Factors related to accessing informal support, culture, the nature of the disability and the child all influenced the type and availability of informal support.

Factors relating to accessibility of support

We found that geographical factors, the partner's employment, availability of child care and frailty of grandparents affected the degree to which parents could access informal support.

The practical support available from the extended family was significantly related to how close they lived to the family. The prospect of taking the child on a long journey, often on public transport, deterred parents from taking up offers of having the child for a weekend or more from family who lived some distance away. However, for some parents the knowledge that such support was there, should the occasion arise, was reassuring.

If I got on the 'phone to my sister now and said 'Can I bring Paul [disabled child] up tomorrow?', she'd say 'Yes' without any hesitation at all. She's really good, it's a shame she doesn't live nearer.
(Whitton)

Living close to other family members did not necessarily imply that the parent was well supported. Several parents reported extended family living nearby who had never offered any form of help.

One reason for parents who lived in rural areas not belonging to a parents' support group was because one did not exist locally. This was, to some degree, due to the fact that the child's condition was quite rare. However, if these parents had been living in large cities it is likely that they would have found a local support group.

Whether or not the partner was working also affected the extent of practical support available to the parent. It was only in those families where the partner was not working that it was possible for him to become equally responsible for the care of the child. As well as directly restricting the amount of help a partner can provide, we found that some mothers were careful not to demand too much of their partners in the evenings because of their having to work the next day.

I'm always the first one to get up, because I think 'Well, he's got work tomorrow'. So I tend to get up and see to them [disabled child and sibling].
(Whiting)

A consequence of spending less time caring for the child was that partners did not become familiar with the more skilled aspects of care, such as doing physiotherapy with the child. As a result they were unable, or reluctant, to support the mothers by carrying out these sorts of tasks.

I   What about the physio or the exercises, do you ever do those?

F   Very rarely. It really does frighten me doing it, because you have to pull his legs and I really panic that I'm going to break something and I just can't do it.
(Greenhow)

Sometimes parents need access to childminding in order to enjoy other forms of support, such as attending a support group or going out with friends. One parent had been to only one support group meeting because she knew her husband would not be able to manage the child on his own.

I actually went when she was not being very good at night and I just wanted to get home because I knew Colin would be pulling his hair out with her. I just didn't go from then on.
(Nicholson)

Finally, physical or mental frailty of grandparents affected both how much parents felt able to ask for help and the amount and type of support offered. Parents spoke about grandparents being unable to manage the extra demands caused by the child's condition, such as difficult behaviours or the child's extra physical or personal care needs. This was often compounded by the presence of siblings.

We used to go to the pub every Friday but we lost that. It was my mother-in-law that used to babysit but she finds it difficult with the three of them.
(Walker)

In some cases parents had reached solutions with respect to the grandparent's limitations. In one case the grandmother helped with less demanding household tasks, and in another the child was put to bed early when the grandmother came to babysit in the evenings. There is clearly an issue here about the way support from the extended family may decrease over the years because of the physical demands it imposes. These demands are likely to increase as the child grows older while, at the same time, grandparents are likely to be growing more frail and their ability to help declines.

Cultural factors

Two points arise in relation to cultural factors affecting availability of support. First, none of the parents from minority groups attended, or had heard of, support groups for parents. It may be that there are certain cultural or class factors which influence who hears about and joins a support group. One parent noted that the support group to which she belonged seemed 'ever so middle-class' (Forsyth).

Secondly, all the families from minority groups had family living nearby or shared their home with members of the extended family. That is not to say, however, that the parent received more support because of this. In two of the families the parents, with their partners, were virtually wholly responsible for the care of the child. In the third family the situation was different. The child's aunt was living with the mother, and the maternal grandparents and the child's uncles called at the house frequently. They were able to relieve the mother from looking after the child. The mother saw her family as sharing the role the child's father would have assumed had he been allowed to immigrate.

> My parents, my sister, my brother, they all care for him so much, and what he's missed out on his father's love, he's getting it from them. I don't think I would have survived a day without them. They've helped me through a lot.
> (Mahmood)

Disability factors

The time since the birth or onset of the disability affected availability of support. We found that the emotional support provided by the extended family and friends decreased over time. Once the crisis period has passed and the family moves into the long-term phase of caring for the child, the issue is no longer new to family and friends and emotional support is less available.

> M   Lisa [disabled child] was the first grandchild on both sides of the family so, at first, there was an awful lot of attention. We have had a lot of support from the family, but it's dropping off rapidly.
> I   Why do you think that is?
> M   I sum it up like this: if you have an illness it doesn't last very long. People are concerned, but they're very concerned for a short time only. I think, for them, the problem's becoming quite boring and they don't want to listen any more. Whereas before I could off-load everything on them if I wanted to, now I find if I start they look at me as if to say 'Oh, she's off again, we're going to get it in the neck here', and they look bored.
> (Reeves)

The extent to which parents could use informal sources of support for practical help was also affected by other disability factors. Some parents were reluctant to ask family, friends or neighbours to childmind if the child had speech or behaviour problems. This was either because the parent felt the person would simply not be able to manage the child, or because the child would not be able to communicate basic needs such as wanting to go to the toilet. On the whole these disability factors played a greater role in affecting parents' use of friends and neighbours for support than close members of the family such as grandparents.

Child factors

Finally, in some instances it was child factors which influenced the type of practical support which partners could provide. Some children wanted their mothers when they woke at night.

> ...and it's always 'Mum' he shouts in the night.
> (Loft)

However, sometimes it worked the other way round. One father always washed the child's hair because she would not let the mother do it. In another family the child always wanted to be with her father if he was in the house.

> She loves her Dad, she loves him more than me. If she's on my lap, she cries to go to him. If he's in the house he has got to have her.
> (Reeves)

Barriers to using informal support

Regardless of the objective availability of support, we found certain factors made parents reluctant to use informal support. These can be thought of as barriers to using informal support.

Reciprocation

The extent to which 'give and take' was possible within support-giving relationships influenced parents' use of informal support. Parents were aware that they would be unlikely to be able to return favours. Feeling unable to reciprocate was a very commonly expressed barrier to asking for help from all sources of informal support. It prevented some parents going for help unless they were in a crisis. Alternatively, where parents already used the extended family for regular child care, they were reluctant to ask for more help when the parent just wanted to have a break. Part of this reluctance stemmed from parents' feeling that they would be unable to pay back or return the favour.

> M   It would be nice to have the sort of arrangement with somebody so that I wasn't having to ask favours and feel beholden to people.

I   And is that how you feel when you ask?

M   Very much so.

I   And does that stop you asking?

M   Yes, I would say so, I think it does. Because you're sort of having to ask people to do it for the love of it.

(Forsyth)

Linked to this was a fear of over-burdening relatives, friends and older siblings. This fear can partly be attributed to not wanting to lose friendships by demanding too much support.

They'll think 'Well, what's she rattling on about?'. So quite honestly, I don't really say much to many other friends because I think 'Oh, they'll think I'm just carrying on'.

(Dobson)

It did not have to be the case that parents were already reliant on the extended family for child care to make them feel that they might be over-burdening their relatives. This parent rarely used relatives for child care, but was extremely reluctant to ask for help despite it being offered.

My aunts are very good, they've often said to use them if we needed to. But they've got their families, and I don't want to impose too much.

(Dobson)

Parents were also conscious that uncles, aunts and friends, who were potential sources of support, often had young families too.

I've got another sister who lives in F_____ who's had him for a night for me, but not very often because she's got five children and so I don't feel as though it's fair that she should have Paul [disabled child].

(Whitton)

Similarly one parent had two older children living locally who sometimes looked after the child. However, they had children of their own and the parent was anxious that she did not over-burden them.

If I do need a break my daughter will take him, but it's just that she's got two others and you don't like to put on, that's all.

(Vyner)

This concern reflected that of many parents in relation to the child's future care. Parents were anxious that the child's siblings should not feel obliged to look after the child when the parents were unable to continue doing so.

Family reactions

The reactions of members of the extended family to the child's disability became barriers to using the family as a source of support in a number of ways.

First, a few parents had sought to 'protect' members of the extended family from knowing the full extent of the child's disability. This limited how much parents could use family members for support. One parent whose child had severe behaviour problems only let the grandparents see him when he was behaving well. Consequently, the mother was unable to use relatives as a means of having a break when she most needed it.

> He tends to have to go round when he's behaving himself and when, to be honest, he wouldn't be a problem being here. (Forsyth)

A number of parents reported that the grandparents had found the child's disability very difficult to accept. As a result parents felt they could not use grandparents as a source of emotional support. More specifically, one couple had decided not to reveal the severity of their child's physical condition to the grandparents to save upsetting them. The mother missed the emotional support she would have got from her own parents.

> M   It would break my mum's heart to know how stiff she'd been some mornings. So we always make sure that whenever they see her she's moving well.
>
> I   Do you think you miss the support that your mother could offer you?
>
> M   Yes, definitely. Sometimes there have been screaming points and I think 'Oh, I wish there was someone here to help'.
> (Davies)

Secondly, although parents did not experience what would be described as overtly negative reactions to the disabled child, parents disliked their child being treated as 'special' by members of the extended family.

> My mum's husband really aggravates me because he treats her [disabled child] different to the other grandchildren and I don't like that. I want her treated as the same as the other grandchildren. He treats her nice in a different way, but it's still singling her out in my mind.
> (Whiting)

Another parent found that grandparents made allowances for the child on account of the disability. This hampered the parent's own efforts to bring the child up to be as independent as possible.

> We make her [disabled child] do things even when she doesn't want to, she's got to learn. But she's bright enough to know that Grandma or certain people will help her even though they know that they shouldn't.
> (Thompson)

Finally, one child's grandparents believed the cause of the child's behaviour problems was the way he had been brought up. This made the parent reluctant to use the grandparents for child care as it was likely to create more stress than it resolved, and also resulted in the possibility of exposing the child to inappropriate disciplining.

> We get situations where, especially during holidays, I'll get vibes from my mother that I'm not doing it right. She'll try and take over and Richard [disabled child] will react, he'll go off the rails and we lose him completely and then she washes her hands of him. So you can't win either way. It's either you're doing wrong, or your child is so badly behaved, and it's your fault anyway. At the end of the day, they're your parents and you're looking to them for support for yourself and when it's not there, you can feel a bit bitter.......That's another bone of contention with my mother. I caught her slapping him [disabled child] once and I was very angry.
> (Walker)

Parents' coping mechanisms

The ways parents had chosen to cope with having a disabled child could act as a barrier to using informal support. One way of coping adopted by parents was to maintain a life which was separate from the disabled child. Parents with friends who predated the birth of the disabled child often chose not to involve these friends too closely with the disabled child. As a result they could not use them as a source of emotional support.

> They'll always ask 'How's Debbie?' and nine times out of ten I'll just say 'Fine'.
> (Davies)

One mother referred to friends she had had before the birth of her disabled child as 'my friends that are nothing to do with Lisa' (Reeves). These friends helped her to maintain a part of her life that was hers. The time spent with those friends was quite different to how she socialised with other parents of disabled children.

> If I go out with my friends that are nothing to do with Lisa, I prefer to go in a situation like the pictures where I haven't got to sit and talk. Whereas if we go to the pub, I prefer to be with people that I can talk about Lisa and they're in the same situation.
> (Reeves)

For some parents there was clearly a conflict between the need for practical and emotional support and the need to maintain a life beyond that of being the parent of a disabled child. The parents in this study appeared, in the main, to have opted for the latter. Similarly, in order to prevent the child's disability dominating her life one parent chose not to join the local support group. She preferred to spend what spare time she had with friends.

Finally, the parent's personality affected whether a parent belonged to a support group. Two parents clearly felt that they were not the sort of people who belonged to groups, and it was for this reason that they had not pursued membership of a support group although they knew of their existence.

> I   Do you belong to any support group for parents?
> M   No, no....I did at the very beginning but I'm not one for...I don't like groups and things like that.
> (Whitton)

Summary

- A number of sources of informal social support were identified including partners, siblings, members of the extended family, friends, neighbours and other parents of disabled children. The support provided by these various groups differed.

- The greatest source of practical and emotional support was the parent's partner.

- Support from the extended family was generally of a practical nature and the level of support varied considerably. It mainly consisted of child care though there were instances of help with household tasks. A number of factors were found to influence the availability of support from the extended family.

- Friends whom parents had known prior to the birth or diagnosis of the disabled child offered very little support to parents. This was partly because parents perceived a number of barriers to using them as a source of support.

- Contact with other parents of disabled children came through local parent support groups as well as through the child attending nursery or school. These parents were a unique source of information and emotional support.

- It was rare to find parents using neighbours as a source of informal support. However, in one or two instances the help provided by a neighbour was very important to the parent. In both cases the support was provided when unexpected difficulties or demands on the parent arose.

- The type and availability of informal support was affected by geographical factors, frailty of grandparents, partner's employment status, access to child care, cultural, disability and child factors.

- Barriers to using informal support included fear of over-burdening, feeling unable to reciprocate, family reactions to the disability and parents' chosen coping mechanisms.

Support from services

Families caring for a disabled child may receive a range of services. These can be grouped according to for whom and for what function they are provided. Thus there are disability services (such as physiotherapy, speech therapy), child support services (such as school), and parent support services (such as respite care, social workers). This distinction is, however, of limited use for a number of reasons. First, some services, such as general practitioners or schools, are used by all children. However, if the child is disabled it is likely that such services become more involved with the child, are more specialised, and have a qualitatively different role in which both child *and* parent are supported. Secondly, some services are explicitly provided with the aim of helping both parent and child, such as child development centres, Portage workers (or pre-school teachers) and health visitors. Thirdly, other services, such as social work, although only ostensibly working with one member of the family, have the effect of supporting the whole family. Finally, as Twigg (1992) showed, carers can also experience support indirectly through the provision of a support service for the disabled person.

This chapter will explore how services supported, or did not support, parents. We emphasise the extent to which the support needs of parent and child are inextricably entwined and focus on the ways in which child-focused and parent-focused services can be support resources for a parent caring for a disabled child. Given the small sample size and the geographical distribution of the families involved, it would not be appropriate to consider the effectiveness of various services or practices. In addition, since we had no knowledge of local service provision other than that gleaned from the parents, it is not possible to comment on use or non-use of local services.

We begin with a brief overview of the formal support services used by these parents before examining sources of stress in services, the ways in which child-focused and parent-focused services met need, and the barriers to their use.

Use of formal support services
An overview of the range of professionals in contact with the families is summarised in Table 3. The high frequency of contact

with health visitors shown in the table is expected since many of the children were less than five years old. Contact with services related to the disability, such as consultants and physiotherapists, were the next most frequent. Very few parents were using what could be regarded as parent support services, such as a social worker.

Table 3:   Formal support used by/available to parents

Professional	No. parents receiving service
Health visitor	9
Physiotherapist	9
Consultant	7
Social worker	4
Child development centre	3
General practitioner	3
Portage worker	3
Adviser from voluntary sector	2
Speech therapist	2
Respite care	
– using service	2
– awaiting placement	2
Community nurse	1
Community mental handicap team key worker	1
Community occupational therapist	1
District nurse	1

The apparently low level involvement of services with these families should not be interpreted as meaning that services had only a minor effect on parents' lives. Services could, in fact, have a pivotal role. The effect a change might have on access to services for the child often influenced decisions. For example, one family was considering whether or not to move house. That decision was being deferred until the family was happy with the child's education placement, despite the fact that the parent was finding their current home increasingly unsuited to looking after a child with severe and complex disabilities. Thus satisfaction with service provision related to one aspect of a child's care affects the ease with which other care needs are met. Furthermore, trying to meet the various needs of the child and family is made more difficult as the quality and level of service provision is largely beyond parents' control.

Perceived needs
It is important to note early in this chapter that, in some cases, it was parents' perceived need for support which was the main factor affecting use of services. Some parents' expectations with regard to having a break from child care did not differ from those of parents

of non-disabled children, especially where the disabled child was quite young.

> We don't go out every week because we want to be with the children. We've had our times of going out before the children came along.
> (Davies)

> I tend to look at it that even if Amanda didn't have Down's syndrome we probably still wouldn't go out.
> (Whiting)

In addition, a few parents did not feel they needed or wanted a break from caring for their child. It was the parents of children with physical disabilities who were still quite independent with respect to self-care who expressed this sentiment.

> Everybody's moaning about the summer holidays starting. I said 'I don't mind, you're not getting up in the morning, rushing about, dashing off, you can take the day leisurely'. And he's no bother, I don't know I've got him. I enjoy having him at home. He's my life at the moment.
> (Vyner)

Services as a source of stress
Services had an impact on parents' ability to cope where they were a source of additional stress. Inadequacy of provision and consequent conflict with service providers were major sources of stress.

Inadequate service provision
Inadequate service provision included actual insufficiencies in the level of provision as well as incompetence or ineptitude in the way a service was being provided. Inadequate service provision often supplanted the emotional distress or physical strain caused by disability-related stresses.

> I   What are the really big problems for you?
> M   I think it tends to change. In the first six months it was just coping with Lisa. She was such a difficult baby. Then not wanting to look towards the future with her ... or thinking of any type of future really for her. But now, I wouldn't say the emotional side of it. I've accepted Lisa for what she is and I love her for what she is. All that has tended to go into the background. Now I find that I just seem to be fighting everybody and everything to get what is right for Lisa. And that is the battle now. Dealing with people and standing up for what you think is right, what she should be having.
> (Reeves)

Parents who were caring for a child with either learning difficulties or severe behaviour problems often felt that their child's needs were not being fully addressed by the medical profession. Since these children did not have any acute medical needs and there was no treatment for the condition, they were usually discharged from the care of a consultant. However, this left parents feeling bitter and isolated.

> She [consultant] just said she's got severe learning difficulties and that was it, basically she said 'goodbye'. And until I went to sort out a school there was basically nothing [in terms of professional input] at all.
> (Dobson)

Parents also perceived inadequacies in services when the level of expertise they expected from a professional was not forthcoming. Few parents felt that their health visitor had any particular skills or knowledge in relation to disabled children.

> To be honest, she's [health visitor] a lovely person and it's nice to have a chat but that's about it. Health visitors right from the start have been absolutely useless: no idea whatsoever. I was very badly misinformed at the start by a health visitor who frightened the living daylights out of me.
> (Reeves)

Inadequacies in services can also be viewed in terms of how quickly services respond to parents' needs. One family was experiencing numerous delays with respect to their application for a social services grant for a ground floor extension. The parents had not anticipated that the process would take so long and the mother was having to carry an increasingly heavy child upstairs. Coupled with this was the anxiety that the extension would not be ready when the child's condition had deteriorated to such an extent that to care for him properly would require the various adaptations and specialist equipment.

A crucial time for parents with a disabled child comes at the time of diagnosis. Health visitors were often involved with parents whose child's disability had not been apparent at birth or had appeared since birth. However, some parents felt let down because their health visitor failed to visit them after the diagnosis had been made.

> As soon as she was diagnosed blind the health visitor didn't show up once. She was totally out of her league.
> (Thompson)

Being let down by formal services may add to the burden of distress already felt by parents. It may also discourage or delay parents from approaching formal support services in the future.

Finally, not all parents were positive about their encounters with medical professionals. Parents spoke of feeling inadequate as a result of consultations or clinic visits, or anger over the consultants' attitude to the child and their condition.

> ...and all these doctors looking down their noses and thinking you're simple. Sometimes I wish some of them did have children with special needs so they'd understand. Because the kids aren't just specimens. And that's what I feel like he's treated sometimes, so I don't enjoy taking him.
> (Carver)

Conflict with service providers

Conflict with service providers, especially those from the education department, was one of the greatest sources of stress for some parents. Dissatisfaction with educational provision for the child, the process of assessing of the child's special educational needs, and negotiating with local education authorities were all extremely wearing and distressing.

> We got him in at the nursery down here because we thought he should have a more controlled environment. And that's when the battle started really. We've had to fight. We've won one-to-one at school, and I'm fighting to keep that.
> (Walker)

> The education authority are the worst. They're obstructive. They're not only unco-operative, they're positively obstructive.
> (Hodder)

Support from school

We have already described how the level and quality of service provision for the child can be an enormous source of stress to parents. The extent to which a parent feels supported by services is as much (if not more) a product of satisfaction with services for the *child* as with satisfaction with *parent* support services. In order to illustrate this point we will take as an example the ways in which, if perceived to be satisfactory, school can support the parent. Through this we shall challenge the notion that education services meet only the child's needs. We shall demonstrate the extent to which education services can both overtly support the parent and also indirectly enhance feelings of being supported.

School can be regarded as a form of respite care. Indeed one parent referred to school using these terms. What makes it different from other types of respite care is that it is 'legitimate'. It is an acceptable means of having a break from child care and it benefits the child as well. No parent expressed any qualms about sending their child to school. It was regarded as a safe place for their child and one which the child enjoyed and benefited from.

It's a lovely school, it really is a lovely school. The teacher and the helpers – they genuinely care for the children. So I've got no fears of her being ill-treated or anything like that.
(Dobson)

Often it was parents whose children had only recently started school who were most conscious of the sense of release, as they were able to indulge in activities, however simple, that they had previously given up.

Especially going to town, taking his pushchair, then he'll struggle to get out of the pushchair and run off. You couldn't do it, you couldn't go round looking at things slowly. It's a bit better now since he's going to school, I can do those things.
(Mahmood)

Some parents relied on the school teaching the child certain skills such as potty-training.

Luckily she's been accepted into a school in September and that's one of the first things they'll try and sort out – her potty-training. I've tried, but as soon as I put her on the potty she absolutely screams. So rather than frighten her off, I'd rather the professionals teach her, because she's not going to want to do anything if I start frightening her.
(Nicholson)

This mother also envisaged that school would tire her child more thereby easing the difficulties of settling the child at night which currently involved one or two hours crying every night before she fell asleep. In other cases it was the child's social development which had made life at home easier.

I   Have you seen an improvement since he's been going there?
M   Oh yes, he's a lot better.
I   Has it made it easier having him here as well?
M   Oh yes, he gets on with other children better. He never used to have anything to do with them at all. Now they will play.
(Walker)

School could also offer a less apparent, but equally important, form of support. Parents who were satisfied with their child's schooling felt supported because other individuals were doing their best to help the child. This relieved parents from the sense that they were alone in trying to give their child the best chance in life.

They've [education authority] been very good. Even as far as dimmer switches, curtains to cut out the light, whatever we need they've got him. They've been very good.
(Vyner)

A number of parents found the interest of school staff in the child and a desire to help the child very supportive.

Before he'd been at another mainstream school, and they were absolutely awful. They weren't understanding at all. But the one he's at now is a lot better and I think that's taken quite a bit of the pressure off us, because they're more willing to cope.
(Forsyth)

This sense of support achieved by having common goals was also found in relation to other education professionals, including educational psychologists and teaching assistants.

They're very good there, they're very keen, they're very interested, especially B _____ and the nursery nurse. She's borrowed a lot of our books to read on the subject which is very good.
(Walker)

Finally, school could be a source of pleasure for parents. Parents enjoyed the child's progress at school, whether in academic, social or life skills. One mother described her joy at seeing her son at school, sitting at a desk wearing the school uniform. It was something she never imagined her child would be able to do and was an indicator of normality and hope.

Parent support through other child services
So far we have examined in some detail the way schools can support parents despite the fact that they are traditionally perceived as a child-focused service. A number of other services provided to meet the child's needs were also found to be supporting the parent in some way. In most cases this was not because it was part of the professional's role to support the parent. It was, rather, the product of the relationship which had developed between the parent and the professional. Because of this the professionals whom parents found supportive varied, depending on personal characteristics, as opposed to professional skills or responsibilities.

Practical and emotional support
Physiotherapists, district nurses, general practitioners, health visitors, consultants and Portage workers were all mentioned by one or more parents as being important sources of both practical and emotional support which went beyond what might be expected

from professionals. The practical support was often in terms of information about local services, benefits or accessing other services.

> My health visitor was absolutely brilliant. She organised moving hospitals, she arranged for the physio to come, she's been chasing up the buggy and she's been talking to me about schools for Ian.
> (Currey)

In some cases the sense of being supported arose from parents feeling that the professional was as concerned about their child as they were. For two parents, the commitment of hospital staff, particularly the consultant, to the child's case was enormously encouraging.

> Because you see how determined they are not to let it get the better of her, that's another reason why doing the exercises isn't always such a chore. Because if they can be bothered to care like that then so can we.
> (Davies)

In other cases the emotional support provided by professionals was simply in terms of being available if the parent needed someone to talk to. Sometimes just knowing support was there if needed was enough. One parent for example had never actually telephoned her child's physiotherapist, although invited to do so.

> We've made good friends with the physios especially Mrs T _____ who has actually given us her home 'phone number in case we get worried or anxious about something, she's there at the end of the 'phone.
> (Davies)

A few parents used a professional as a regular source of emotional support. In one instance, the district nurse, who called three times a week, was the main source of emotional support for an extremely isolated parent. Another parent, although dissatisfied with the extent to which her health visitor could offer practical help, found her an important source of emotional support.

> I   And how often does your health visitor come?
> M   When I 'phone, which isn't as much now as I used to. Because at the end of the day she's limited to what she can do. She's just an ear really.
> (Walker)

Empowerment
Three of the pre-school children had a Portage worker who visited the home about once a week. The parents could not speak highly

enough of this service. Because the Portage workers visited frequently and regularly, they were often the first professional with whom the parent discussed a problem. Portage has sometimes been criticised as placing another burden on parents who are expected to work at set tasks with the child between visits (Turnbull, 1985; Appleton and Minchom, 1991). However, we did not find this and indeed parents said that they welcomed and appreciated the opportunity to learn how they could best help their child.

> We've had a wonderful service from Portage. We could never thank them enough for what they've given us; the opportunity to sort of realise that your child can do something that you don't think they can do. And at an early age. We started doing things with her earlier than we would have thought that she was able to cope with. By introducing them early she's sort of come to do them at the normal stages.
> (Whiting)

The attitudes of professionals to the parental role could also serve to empower parents. Two parents recalled clearly what their consultant had said to them at the time of diagnosis. In both cases it had become central to their attitudes and approach to the care of the child.

> I cornered one the doctors and said 'Look, give us some advice on education – what do you think?'. He said to me 'There's no point you asking me, I'm just a doctor. When it comes to that child you are the expert. You are the person who knows what is best for your child, and don't let anyone tell you otherwise'. And that went home, and I thought 'Right..', you know.
> (Thompson)

Use of parent support services
Social workers, respite care and home helps are parent-focused services used to support parents in their role as carers. Although regarded as parent-focused, these services differ in the way support is achieved. Social workers and home helps, for example, work with or help the *parent*, but it is the *child* who actually receives respite care.

Four parents were in contact with a social worker, though the extent of the social worker's involvement varied. Two mothers had contact with a social worker on an irregular basis. In one case a social worker at the special needs nursery had helped the mother to sort out respite care for her child. The second mother resisted more social worker involvement, regarding too much help from social services as a threat to her independence. The two mothers who were in regular contact with a social worker were extremely satisfied with the help provided. This included advice concerning benefits, housing rebates and other support offered by social services. Both parents also valued knowing support would be available when they needed it – either by telephone or by seeing the social worker at the Parents' Advisory Centre. The fact that this level of support *was* available gave one mother the confidence to try to manage any difficulties herself before turning to professional help.

> I feel in a situation like that, you could become vulnerable to letting go, sitting back and letting everybody else do the bloody work. Like the social workers have said 'Anything you need, give us a ring'. And like for this rent rebate, I thought 'I'll go about sorting it myself first' and then it got difficult and I thought 'Right, I'll call them [social workers] in now 'cause I do need them'.
> (Abbott)

The sense of help being available when it was needed did not apply only to information or advice. This mother also felt that support would be there if she could no longer manage to care for her child.

> If ever it was getting to me and I thought Angela would be in any danger, I'd hand her over. I'd have her in before I got to that stage.
> (Abbott)

However, despite regular contact with their social workers, neither mother regarded them as sources of emotional support. Both were in contact with other parents of children with disabilities, and they preferred to confide in them.

> We [parent and social worker] have a chat from time to time. If I want to go and talk to her, I can go and talk to her. But I don't because I have the other mothers. Carol's a social worker, she hasn't got a child with special needs. I know she comes into contact with them, but she hasn't got one.
> (Carver)

Respite care

When we visited the families for the first interview, only two parents were actually using a respite care service, although a number of other parents were aware of them and talked about why they were not currently using them. One parent had belonged to the Link-a-Family scheme for two years. She used this service in the school holidays when the link family had the disabled child to stay for one or two days a week. The second parent had been provided with a respite care worker just two months before we visited. At this early stage the child was still getting to know the worker who visited once a fortnight. The parent envisaged that, in the future, she would use the service when she had appointments and when she and her husband wanted to go away overnight. A further two parents had applied for a local respite service and intended to use it once it had been arranged. Both involved finding a suitable link family, and one parent had been waiting for two and a half years. Finally, two other parents had placed their child's name on a respite care scheme but did not intend to use it for a number of years.

There were a variety of factors which had precipitated parents' decisions to use, or apply to use, respite care. The needs of siblings was a common reason. One parent vividly remembered the events which precipitated her decision to apply for respite care.

> We were walking down the High Road and Susan [sibling] was trying to tell me this story, but Paul [disabled child] was there and he takes over, and she said 'Do you know what mum, he destroys all communication in this house'. And it was when Peter [sibling] asked me to go off shopping and I couldn't go [because of disabled child], I thought this is really unfair on the other two.
> (Whitton)

Parents felt that using respite care would enable both of them to spend time with their other children, and give the siblings a break from the disabled child.

> Although they get on well together my other daughter needs a break from her just as much as the rest of us do. And it's nice to have a couple of days when we can hire a video, or we can do things together like baking. Things we couldn't do with Jenny around.
> (Hodder)

Also, parents themselves felt the need to have a break. One parent had found that childminding support from the family was declining and, as a result, felt that she would need to use formal services.

> I've always known that it's [respite care] been there but I've just never felt I've had the need because of the support from the family. But with that dropping off now, I think if it drops off much more I'm definitely going to need some type of break from it.
> (Reeves)

Another parent felt that having a break would give her more time for herself, and enable her to re-establish her identity after three years of providing intensive therapy and care. Other parents put it more simply: they sometimes hit 'rock bottom' and they needed a break to prevent this happening. Finally, where there was no spouse support, the availability of child care was often limited. For these parents respite care offered the opportunity to have a break.

> And it makes it hard being on my own because I haven't got anybody to say to 'Right Dad, take them away for an hour'.
> (Currey)

Home helps
One mother paid for social services 'Home Care' once a week to do the family's ironing. Keeping on top of the ironing had been a particular strain for this mother, so release from this task had been extremely beneficial.

> We were getting to the stage where we've never got any clothes to wear, they were always on the ironing pile. It was always one of those jobs that can wait. But eventually that starts to wear you down. It [having the ironing done for me] has made a really big difference.
> (Reeves)

The support offered by social services was not always viewed as being particularly helpful. One mother used to have help with housework but that had been withdrawn. Instead, the help offered by social services centred on the care of the child, which was not the sort of support the mother needed.

> They'll send someone round to bath her or dress her, but there's no point in that 'cos my husband's here when I'm doing that.
> (Hodder)

Resistance to use of support services
The extent to which parent support services were used was constrained by a number of factors. In some cases, a misunderstanding of the role of a support service made parents reluctant to use it. This was especially found with regard to social workers. One parent thought that enlisting the help of a social worker would threaten her independence. Another associated a visit from a social worker with the risk of children being taken into care.

> I tend not to be involved with social workers 'cos all you hear is bad stories. I was amazed when Carol [hospital social worker] came round and was telling me I was looking after my children properly, when you hear that they're ready to drag your kids out of the door.
> (Carver)

More general concerns about using a parent support service included the degree to which parents felt a service would meet their needs, and the perceived implications of using or approaching services.

Suitability of services
The help most often needed by parents did not require someone with special training or qualifications. Often it was merely to have someone to occupy or play with the child while the parent got on with something else. Such help is not available through formal sources and parents were dependent on informal support.

More specifically, if parents felt a support service was inappropriate for them or their child they would not use it. This was particularly found in relation to use of respite care services. Three parents had chosen not to use respite care because it was not suitable for their child in some way.

> She did go once or twice to the respite care centre at school but she used to come home very disturbed and unhappy from that. (Hodder)

> The only thing that concerns me about her going there is the equipment. It was originally set up as respite for mentally handicapped children and it's only in the last couple of years that they've started taking physically disabled. They have said they're going to try and buy equipment but I will be worried about her when she's there if she's not got the correct seating. (Reeves)

Other parents were looking for a more flexible respite care service, and one which did not involve institutional care.

> I would want somebody who'd come out to your house and work with you to give you exactly what you wanted. (Forsyth)

Furthermore, parents were not prepared to use respite care if they felt that the child would be unable to cope with the separation from home and family. Where the service involved the child going away some parents thought their child was too young.

> I was given a respite care worker over a year ago, but we actually had to take Caroline to her and she was going through that clinging stage. There was no way I could leave her, no way. (Nicholson)

For children with intellectual impairments or behavioural difficulties, the issue of when they are ready or able to cope with respite care is exacerbated. This parent's child had severe behavioural problems and it was difficult to predict what would cause a decline in the child's behaviour.

> Mark is pretty much on a level at the moment, progressing nicely, things seem to be fairly stable. I wouldn't want to risk that by going into it [respite care] at the moment.
> (Forsyth)

Finally, a number of parents were resistant to the idea of professionals coming into the home to help them with the care of the child or therapies. They felt that the benefits of such help would be outweighed by the ways it might constrain and impinge on normal family activities.

Perceived implications of using/approaching services

Parents perceived a certain amount of stigma to be attached to using a parent support service. This was linked both to feelings of failure and parents' perception of the role of a service. One parent, who had no previous contact with social workers, felt that it would be highly stigmatising to need help from one.

> I don't know anyone that's a social worker. I've never had anything to do with social workers. You always hear that bad families..not a bad family but less fortunate families have social workers. You think 'Oh God, that's terrible I could never have one of them'. I suppose I was thinking 'I'm too good to have a social worker'.
> (Loft)

Using a parent support service such as help with care tasks or therapies was seen by some parents as an indication of failure or of being no longer able to cope.

> We don't have a lot of people coming in to help. If someone came in and helped to put him to bed, then that wouldn't be normal. We cope on our own. That's how we keep it sort of normal.
> (Greenhow)

Similarly, using respite care was seen by some parents in terms of failing as a parent and also failing the child.

> It makes you feel like you're giving up. You feel like you're giving up on your own child. I know it's ridiculous but you do. It's your child, you should be able to cope, he needs you and all the rest of it.
> (Walker)

These feelings either made it very difficult for parents to make use of a respite service or from considering respite care as an option.

I don't want him in respite care or anything like that because he's my son, he's my responsibility. I don't believe in shoving him off.
(Carver)

Parents were not only conscious of their own feelings of failure, but were sensitive to the ways other people might react to their decision to use a support service. One parent who was considering using respite care was clearly anxious about her family's reaction, and this was making what was already a difficult decision for her even harder.

My husband and I do disagree with that. I'm more prepared to let him go than he is. He's not prepared to let him go. I'm not fully happy with it, but I'm with him more so I hit rock bottom a lot more than my husband does. And I can't ever imagine telling my mother [about using respite care], she'd go nuts.
(Walker)

Summary

- The service needs of the child are paramount to parents. If services for the child are felt to be inadequate or unsatisfactory it can be a major source of stress for parents. In contrast, satisfaction with child-focused services left parents feeling supported in caring for their child. Such services could also meet some of the parents' emotional needs.

- Experiences of being let down by services, conflicts with service providers and unacceptable attitudes among professionals were some of the ways parents found services to be unsupportive.

- Some needs of parents were met indirectly through contact with professionals providing help to the child. This was the product of the relationship which developed between parent and professional, and offered emotional and practical support to the parent.

- Use of parent support services was low and was constrained by misunderstandings about the role of support services, the suitability of services for both parent and child, and the perception that using or approaching services was an indication of failure and 'not coping'.

Financial and material resources

Families caring for a disabled child are at greater risk of financial disadvantage because of the likely impact on earnings of having a disabled child together with the so-called extra costs caused by the disability (Baldwin, 1985; Smyth and Robus, 1989). Research has shown that money and other material resources are important factors in alleviating or preventing stress in mothers caring for a disabled child (Wallander et al., 1989; Quine and Pahl, 1991; Sloper and Turner, 1993).

Our study included both parents on very low incomes and those with higher living standards where there was a regular income. It was clear that, for some, poverty was sometimes as big a problem as the disability. However, this research was not a study of poverty, or even poverty and disability. Instead we focused on how parents were able to use disability benefits and material resources to help them care for their child.

Attitudes to disability benefits
All parents welcomed the benefits they received and spoke in general way about the way the extra money helped them.

> I   Do you find the money helps at all?
> M   Oh yes, it brings smiles to our faces rather than struggle.
> (Nicholson)

Some parents had felt guilty about receiving benefits, especially when they first started receiving them. However, all were aware of the extra costs of caring for their child especially as the child grew older.

> I've always felt guilty having the allowances I get. I feel I'm being paid to bring up my own child.
> (Nicholson)

Disability benefits were seen by some parents as a form of compensation. Entitlement to benefits was regarded by these parents as an acknowledgement by the state of the particular difficulties and problems associated with caring for and bringing up a disabled child.

> It's a very, very small compensation.
> (Walker)

I feel that because it's such a strain we deserve to have that bit extra.
(Whitton)

For one parent, however, being eligible for disability benefits had negative connotations in that it meant admitting there was something wrong with her child.

We got it [DLA] first time, which was good and bad. It was good that we got it, but it was confirmation that something was wrong.
(Walker)

Use of disability benefits

Parents tended to treat the benefits they received as a lump sum. They were not always able to separate, for instance, how they spent the care component of the disability living allowance[2] (DLA) as opposed to the mobility component.

Parents differed in their use of disability benefits. Families on a very low income often found that these benefits became absorbed into the general household budget and the task of trying to make ends meet. Benefits were however also seen as something extra that would help parents to meet needs that they would not otherwise have been able to afford for their child.

We also get an attendance allowance for Angela. We get a full one [higher rate] for that which was good. That's helped because if she needs anything I can go out and get it for her.
(Abbott)

Families with a regular, if modest, income often viewed the disability benefits as extra money which had specifically helped them overcome certain difficulties. These parents were better able to use the money both to meet the extra costs incurred as a result of the disability and to ease the strains and burden of care.

Using benefits to meet disability-related costs

Meeting extra transport costs was the most common use of disability benefits both for parents who were receiving the mobility

---

[2] The disability living allowance was introduced in April 1992, replacing the attendance allowance and mobility allowance. It is an non-contributory, non-means-tested benefit. It has two components. The *care component* is paid at three different rates according to the care needs of the disabled person, the frequency of care needs and whether the person needs care at night. For children, it must be shown that the supervision and care needed is greater than would be required by a non-disabled child of the same age. The *mobility component* is paid if the person needs help getting about. There is a lower age limit of five years. It is paid at two rates. The new lower rate is paid where the person, although mobile, has either severe physical or mental impairments which result in the need for guidance or supervision from another person most of the time when out and about.

component of the DLA *and* those who were not. Some had used their benefits to help them buy a car or to cover running costs. One parent who did not receive any mobility benefits had used back payments of her invalid care allowance[3] (ICA) to buy a car. This had made an enormous difference to her life. Her child did not suffer from mobility problems *per se,* but severe behavioural problems had made it extremely difficult for the parent to go out with the child and his two siblings. Another parent tended to use taxis rather than public transport because of her child's severe social and communication impairments. Since she had only been awarded the lower rate of the mobility component of the DLA, she found she was using the care component of the DLA to pay for taxi hire. She questioned the criteria by which decisions about rates for mobility allowances were decided.

> Apparently we stand little or no chance of receiving mobility at the full rate. But a kid with Mark's problems is so hard or harder to take out than probably a kid in a wheelchair. Apparently you stand a chance of getting a higher rate if you're on the high rate attendance allowance that covers nights. But your kid might sleep every night of the week and still be a sod to take out basically.
> (Forsyth)

Regardless of the nature of the disability, transport costs for families living in rural or isolated areas are likely to be increased. One parent had regular trips of 20 miles or so for hospital appointments and physiotherapy. The playgroup the child attended twice a week was over four miles away. As the child was not eligible for the mobility component of the DLA, the mother found she used the care component to cover the additional travel costs. It could be argued she could use the transport services which were provided, but she felt that the transport was either unsafe or meant that the child was away from home for an extremely long time.

> They do have a minibus for opportunity group. I suppose if I did want to use the bus they would probably detour and pick us up. But I don't like going on minibuses with small children because you can't strap them in, whereas I find they're secure in the car. She could use the ambulance to go to physiotherapy, but then it would mean that she'd be out for five hours. The session starts at 1.30 and the ambulance would pick her up at 12 o'clock

---

[3] The invalid care allowance is a non-contributory non-means tested benefit paid to and claimed by the carer. It can be claimed by people of working age who are looking after another person who is receiving either the medium or high rate care component of the DLA. To be eligible the person must not be working full-time or earning more than £40 per week, and they must be caring for the person for at least thirty-five hours a week.

because it takes time to go round and pick everybody up. Coming back would be the same, she probably wouldn't get home until five-ish.
(Whiting)

Some parents were using disability benefits to buy equipment which they felt should be met by statutory services. One parent was using the care component of the DLA to purchase a proper chair for her child with cerebral palsy.

I   Is there any specific thing that you've found that money would be useful for?

M   Yes, equipment for Lisa, we've had terrible problems with getting equipment. The only thing actually that the authority has bought for her is the standing frame. When it comes to chairs we've actually had to purchase those for ourselves. So there has been a lot of added expense considering the chairs are about £400. It's quite a lot of money to find just to seat a child.
(Reeves)

In other cases parents used benefits to buy equipment or other items which, though less essential, were important to the child's comfort, safety or happiness. They included clothing, a car seat suitable for older children and satellite television (this child was confined to a wheelchair).

Finally there were disability-related expenses particular to each family's circumstances. For parents living in urban areas where there were no suitable playgrounds, disability benefits helped towards meeting the cost of taking their child out. Sometimes this was just driving to a park, but on other occasions the trips were more expensive. Being able to take the child out relieved the strain of occupying a demanding child indoors. One parent used part of her benefits to cover the cost of taking the child to a playgroup which was set up for children with special needs. This group was twice as expensive as the local playgroup and involved an eight mile round trip by car. Another parent paid part of the care component of the DLA and her own ICA into an endowment scheme for her child because she was particularly worried about what would happen to her child as she [the parent] grew older. She found the process of putting this money aside served to relieve some of these anxieties, although was doubtful if the money would actually be of any help.

Using benefits to meet the parents' needs
Both the extra disability-related costs and the often poor living circumstances of these families meant that few parents were able to

use disability benefits to meet any of their own needs related to the care of their child.

Two parents did use some of their benefits to pay for help with housework. One mother paid for someone to do the ironing which relieved her of something which had become a considerable source of strain. The second used a home-help in the holidays when the child was at home all day.

One single parent used the benefits to employ a live-in nanny to care for her children. This mother was self employed and was setting up a business from home. Although her financial situation was precarious, the mother felt the only way she could manage was to pay for full-time help.

Finally, for one family the disability benefits had meant that the mother did not have to work full time. She had a part-time job which she enjoyed because it gave her a set of interests separate from her home life. Her child was, however, severely physically disabled by a degenerative muscular condition and she needed (and wanted) to be at home when the child returned from school.

The Family Fund
The views of parents in this study probably reflect the vast majority of families who have been helped by the Family Fund (Lonsdale, 1978; Bradshaw, 1980; Glendinning, 1986). They had nothing but praise for a system of providing financial and material help which was both personal and extremely efficient.

> I tried them [the Family Fund] and they were fantastic. There was no hanging about, they just get on with it.
> (Carver)

As well as providing a highly regarded service, the Family Fund met what were often fundamental care-related needs. Many families had been able to take a holiday which they could not have afforded without a Family Fund grant. For parents on very low incomes the Family Fund provided vital equipment such as washing machines, tumble dryers and telephones. This made an enormous difference to parents' lives. One mother said she had felt 'a lot better' in herself since the washing machine and dryer had been installed. Such equipment not only relieved the physical burden of hand-washing or going to a launderette, it also helped save money.

> I   And has that made a difference having ...
> M   ...having a washing machine? Definitely! I badly needed one because it was costing a fortune because he still wets the bed.
> (Carver)

It has been clear throughout that many parents found the telephone invaluable in dealing with problems with services, as well as a means of contacting key sources of support, whether family, friends or professionals. For one parent, the provision of a telephone by the Family Fund had also relieved anxieties about dealing with medical crises.

> The one thing I really did want was the 'phone. I am so grateful it is in[stalled] because there have been so many times when using a 'phone box [would have been difficult]. It isn't far, it would take me five minutes to walk it, but what would I do in the middle of the night if Ian's [disabled child] bad? Do I leave him here, do I run down there or take him? I really am grateful for that ['phone].
> (Currey)

A feature of the Family Fund is that it seeks, within reason, to meet particular or individual needs as long as they come under the broad specification of being related to the care of the child. One parent had been able to purchase a monitor for the child's computer using a Family Fund grant. The child, who was extremely difficult to occupy, benefited from this, as did the mother. Other parents had been able to buy a pram or buggy which greatly relieved the problems of getting about with a child who was unable to walk or had to be constantly watched.

> They've given us the money for a holiday this year and for Anna's buggy. As long as she can be in her buggy when we go shopping she's as good as gold.
> (Dobson)

Finally it is important to report that one parent was reluctant to re-apply to the Family Fund because it might mean that someone less well-off might miss out.

> I just think there's probably only so much money in the Fund. They might give it to us because we've got a disabled child, where somebody a lot poorer than us might have to go without.
> (Williams)

Difficulties with the benefits system
Most often difficulties concerned finding out about entitlement to benefits and the process of making applications. It was remarkable that two parents in our study had been without disability benefits for four and eight years respectively. Often parents learned about benefits through informal sources. They recalled being confused about eligibility, often because having a disabled child was their first contact with the benefits system. One parent expressed her

experiences of finding out about her rights and entitlements in the following way.

It's up to you to chase them because they're not going to offer it to you. You don't get the information sent to you. You have to go out and dig for it.
(Carver)

There were other reasons why parents had experienced difficulties as they applied for benefits. Self-employed status made completing application forms particularly difficult.

We could have done without the hassle of what's your profit, and what's this and what's that. It was the last thing on my mind.
(Loft)

Another parent encountered what seemed to be an illogical practice in assessment for the attendance and mobility allowances.

I had to take Alan all the way to the other side of T _____ for the mobility. The doctor came here about the attendance allowance.
(Greenhow)

Satisfaction with benefits

There were differences in how satisfied parents were with the level of benefits they received, depending on the age of the child and the type of disability. Parents of very young children tended to be more satisfied. However, they had not yet encountered some of the extra costs associated with having a disabled child, such as buying equipment, transport and having to make adaptations to the home. Other parents did not feel that their disabled child cost them, in financial terms, any more than non-disabled siblings.

She's no different money-wise to any other child.
(Dobson)

Traditionally, financial disadvantage is talked about in terms of those with very low incomes. However, we found in our study that the higher income families were sometimes disadvantaged. This was particularly the case when applying for a grant which was means-tested.

We found ourselves up against the statutory bodies which wouldn't give us a grant because they means-tested us. I don't object to being means-tested, it's quite fair. But the means-test itself was unfair because it took no account of outgoings. They base it on a mortgage of £14,000. Ours is more than three times that much, and they took no account of the car loan. So on the

basis of the test they said we could afford to pay £5,000 which was absurd.
(Hodder)

Summary

- Parents on very low incomes found that some or all disability benefits tended to be absorbed into the general household purse. These families were unable to consider using the money to ease the burden of care through the purchase of a car, help with housework or childminding.

- Both those receiving the DLA mobility component and those who were not had extra transport costs. Those parents living in rural areas and those with children with severe social and behavioural difficulties who did not receive help with mobility were using other disability benefits to meet sometimes quite substantial transport costs.

- Disability benefits were used mostly to cover the extra costs caused by the disability. There was rarely anything left to meet the parents' own needs in relation to the care of the child. Parents who were able to use disability benefits to relieve the burden of care tasks used the money to pay for help with housework and child care.

- All parents praised the Family Fund and its unique method of administration. In many cases the practical resources provided by the Fund had made an enormous difference to parents' lives.

- Confusion about eligibility, entitlement or simply not knowing about disability benefits had delayed some parents in making applications.

- The difficulty faced by higher income families with respect to receipt of means-tested grants was highlighted.

The role of the child

Research into families with a disabled child has largely ignored the child. By this we do not mean the child's *disability*. Disability indicators such as severity, ability to self-care and behaviour problems have long been shown to be associated with the degree of stress experienced by parents (for example, Bradshaw and Lawton, 1978; Quine and Pahl, 1985). It is essential, however, that research does not regard the child's contribution to the coping process merely in terms of disability factors. In doing so, other factors such as the child's capacity to respond to and love others, their personality, disposition and physical appearance are largely ignored. This is regrettable for two reasons. First, it implies that the research has adapted an essentially 'medical' model of disability, where the focus of attention lies with the deficits or 'abnormalities' of the child. Secondly, and in consequence, an incomplete and inaccurate picture is portrayed which suggests that child factors are insignificant compared to disability factors.

Parents do not view their child as a disability. They describe their child as an individual who has limitations and difficulties arising from the disabling condition.

I   I won't meet Jenny today, perhaps you could describe her to me?

M   She's a pickle! (laughs) She has cerebral palsy with quadriplegia.

(Hodder)

This chapter seeks to redress the imbalance by exploring the role of the child in how parents cope. We found two ways in which child factors affected the coping process. First, they affected the amount of stress faced by the parent; and secondly, they influenced how parents coped with the stresses.

The child's influence on the extent of stress
The degree to which a child accepted disability and the ability to take responsibility for his or her well-being affected the extent of care-related problems facing the parent.

Self-management of the impairment
Children who were able to manage their impairments in some way reduced some of the care burden for the parent. Three parents

described how, as their child was growing older, this shift in responsibility was occurring. Two of the children had learnt the extent to which their disability restricted their lives. One child had albinism and came indoors of his own accord during sunny weather. Indeed this mother envisaged being able to hand over responsibility for applying barrier creams to the child within the year. The other child had arthritis, and had learnt when to rest her joints.

> If she's had enough or something, she will come down and say 'my legs hurt' and then we'll stop. She knows her limits, what she can do and what she can't do and we just take it from there.
> (Davies)

One consequence of children taking such responsibility is the reduced likelihood of arguments between parent and child about when to stop certain activities and so on. The third child was beginning to learn ways of controlling his temper and preventing it from developing into a full-blown tantrum.

> He's found that if he's on his own, he can control it a little bit more. Now he finds he can calm down in his bedroom on his own. Quite often, if he's having a paddy, he'll take himself off up there, which is quite a good thing. Obviously it helps him and it helps us.
> (Forsyth)

Child's response to therapies or treatments

Treatment regimes can be a source of stress and dispute between parent and child (LaGreca, 1988; Eiser, 1990). If a child is reluctant to take medication, or will not do exercises or have physiotherapy, it can become a daily problem for parents and an area of conflict between parent and child. Several parents felt that they were fortunate because their child enjoyed the treatments or investigations necessary to manage the condition. For instance, one young child had hydrotherapy three times a week and also did exercises at home twice a day.

> Fortunately she loves water so going up the hospital is no big problem. And she is good, she will do the exercises.
> (Davies)

Another parent was extremely grateful that her child was fascinated by hospitals. This child was suffering from a degenerative condition and hospital visits to monitor the condition were emotionally sensitive times. The parent was relieved by the child's inquisitive approach to these visits.

> He's a bit inquisitive and he seems to actually enjoy visits to the hospital. They've got the meter thing that they blow into and

everything like that, and he takes all that in, takes an interest in it all so he doesn't find it a strain or a bore. You can get on with it, and he likes meeting different people as well so he loves it. (Greenhow)

Child's response to being disabled

Where the child had accepted the disabling condition there was less demand on the parents to support and counsel the child. It also relieved parents of the distress of seeing their child upset and resisting the reality of their disability.

M   But she's coping very well.
F   Yes, she's probably coped better than we have. She's more or less come to terms with it.
(Davies)

This was especially the case when onset of the condition had occurred in childhood rather than at birth. One parent had been dreading the time when her child would have to start using a wheelchair. In the event it was not at all traumatic and the child handled the situation very well, as he had throughout the course of the illness.

Right from the beginning he's sort of accepted it. Like when he went into a wheelchair, I think it worried us more than it did him. He seemed to accept it as a natural progression, and he was happier once he was in the wheelchair because he wasn't falling over. (Greenhow)

The child's influence on how parents cope

Three sets of child factors were found to influence how parents coped. These were the child's physical appearance, their personality or disposition and the degree to which the child was seen to be overcoming the disability. In various ways these factors affected how parents coped by acting as 'morale boosters', by ensuring that a positive parent-child relationship was maintained and by affecting the availability of support.

Morale booster

As with any child, these disabled children were a real source of pleasure to their parents, which helped to lift parents' spirits and boost their morale.

...but no, it's not all doom and gloom. I wouldn't be without her. She's absolutely lovely, she really is lovely. (Dobson)

Many parents spoke of the ways the child's character and antics made them laugh, and how much they enjoyed the times they played with the child. The relationship between parent and child was clearly two-way, and parents acknowledged the ways their child helped them.

> She gives me a lot at the end of the day, she doesn't need to because I don't expect anything from her.
> (Abbott)

> We get a lot of affection from her and that really is the most important thing. You know she feels love, and she gives love in return and that's terrific.
> (Hodder)

Naturally the children differed in their own characters and temperament. It was striking, however, that the experiences of the three parents who had a Down's syndrome child were similar. All spoke of their child's exuberance and extremely happy disposition. The following description by one parent was typical.

> M   She's very, very comical. She loves to play and laugh and joke. She loves to sing and dance. She gives a great deal of pleasure to everybody around her in that way. She'll have the whole room laughing. Although she has got problems, she has still brought into our world the joy that any other child would bring and more.
> I   What do you mean by more...?
> M   Well, just the fact that there's no end to her ability to enjoy herself.
> (Whiting)

Age may be an important factor here, however. Our study only included young children. What might be endearing behaviour in a young child may be less acceptable in a young disabled adult.

Parents also gained a lot of pleasure from their child's appearance. If the interviewer did not meet the child she was usually shown photographs, and parents were clearly proud of their children. Parents also enjoyed the fact that others found their children attractive and likeable, and how people were drawn to them.

> Everybody is really friendly towards him, everybody loves him.
> (Whitton)

> A lot of people have said how appealing he is and what a nice child he is. It's like a lot of special children they've got their own sort of beauty.
> (Walker)

As well as the pleasures the children gave the parents, the ways the children had adapted to the disability also boosted parents' morale.

As I say, she's very determined. She is really the one that you draw your strength off I'm sure.
(Davies)

This was found both in children whose disability had its onset several years after birth as well as those born with the disabling condition. Sometimes the child's own determination was also a source of hope for the parent.

He might be able to walk but he'll need an aid of some sort. But she [physiotherapist] does feel, because he is such a damn hard trier, she feels he will do it.
(Currey)

In other instances, children's ways of overcoming their impairments were sources of admiration. One mother, who was adamant that her child should attend a mainstream school, was proud to report that the child had 'coped well' and that he would be 'alright.. he'll be able to do it'. Another mother was constantly amazed by the ways her child managed to do various activities.

It must be hard. I've tried it myself – I've tried to pick things up how he does. And he can do, he can get things. He can answer the telephone, believe it or not. How he gets his arm up there I don't know. But he throws them and then he gets it. He'll get it on here and he'll hold it up with his shoulder and this arm. And when he wants to scratch his nose, he'll lift it up with his arm, he'll lift the one arm up, and he'll do it like this. It's amazing what he does.
(Baron)

The quality of the parent-child relationship
Research has shown that disabled children are more likely to have communication difficulties and behaviour problems (Pless and Roghmann, 1971; Quine and Pahl, 1989), both of which can test the relationship between parent and child. However, other qualities of the child can ensure that a close relationship is maintained. An important factor here was the child's sense of humour.

We share a lot of giggles. She's got quite a sense of humour and it's very easy to say the right things to trigger that off, and that brings us closer.
(Hodder)

An affectionate nature was another valued quality. Where the child had severe behaviour problems and could be quite unpredictable and unmanageable, the affection the child could give was very precious and served to maintain good relationships between the child and other family members.

He can be very, very loving; and he has a lot of good relationships with a lot of the members of our family.
(Forsyth)

The child's ability to display affection often seemed to serve the
purpose of relieving a fraught situation or raising spirits. It brought
to the fore parents' fundamental feelings of love towards the child
which the strains and frustrations of day-to-day life sometimes
submerged. One mother described the way her child was able to
calm her down and cheer her up after he had pushed her too far!

> When I get cross with Paul, when he drives you mad, and I
> shout and I say 'Oh, I'm fed up, why don't you do this or do
> that?' and he comes up to me and he says 'Sorry Mummy'. And
> I think 'Oh... you can't, he is just so loving'. He'll come and he'll
> sit by you and you think 'Oh, I wouldn't be without him for the
> world'.
> (Whitton)

The availability of support

Some parents believed that their child's physical appearance or
disposition had influenced the support they received from informal
and formal sources. If the child was affectionate and able to form
good relationships with extended family members, it was easier for
parents to use them for childminding. Two parents, who relied
exclusively on family for child care, regarded this as extremely
important. Another mother was carrying out an intensive physiotherapy programme with her child. Each session required two
helpers, and there were four sessions a day. The fact that her child
was appealing and attractive had made it much easier to find
volunteers to help.

> Because she's quite cute everybody likes to help her and that's
> made it easier. If she was a little horror obviously I'd have
> problems. I don't think people would want to come.
> (Nicholson)

Another parent believed that because his child was attractive and
did not look disabled, it had been significantly easier for him to
persuade the education department to allow her to attend the local
primary school as opposed to sending her away to special school.

> I might be also worth pointing out that Louise actually looks
> like a 'normal' child. She doesn't look blind at all. She has no
> blindisms, and she is a very attractive little girl ... it makes it
> easier that she's pretty and people fall in love with her in the
> education department.
> (Thompson)

It should perhaps be noted here that 'looking normal' is not always an advantage. Parents of children with severe behavioural difficulties found that the absence of any physical manifestation of the problem led members of the public to make incorrect judgements about the child and the parents. As a result the support that might have been offered was not forthcoming.

A family with a child in a wheelchair might get an awful lot of help. Or a child with Down's syndrome who starts creating might get – 'You come to the front, no problem, it doesn't matter'. You get a child like ours, who looks a hundred and ten per cent normal, that's creating and you get 'Look at that family, they can't keep their child under control. He should know better, he should do this'.
(Forsyth)

Summary
- Child factors affecting the extent of stresses experienced by parents include the child's ability to self-manage their impairment, the child's response to therapies or treatments, and the child's response to the impairment.

- These factors alleviated the extent of stress by reducing the number of care tasks, relieving parents of responsibility for certain care tasks and reducing emotional distress brought on by the child's own distress.

- The children's endearing qualities, temperament, looks and their own ability to cope with the impairment served to boost parents' morale.

- The strength and quality of the parent-child relationship contributed to how well a parent managed the stresses of care. Factors such as the child's ability to give and receive affection and share jokes served to strengthen the parent-child relationship.

- Child factors also affected the availability of formal and informal support to parents. Parents believed that the child's ability to form good relationships with other people and physical attractiveness were important factors in relation to the availability of support.

Keeping going

Perhaps the most common reaction on seeing a family with a severely disabled child is to think 'I could never do that, I wouldn't be able to cope'. The lay person sees that family's situation exclusively in terms of the disability and the enormous burdens and difficulties which parents may be facing. Researchers have been equally guilty of taking this perspective. Families with disabled children have been pathologised by researchers and practitioners, and seen as deviating from notions of what constitutes a normal family (Byrne, Cunningham and Sloper, 1988). Implicit in this approach is the assumption that family bonds, emotions and feelings do not exist in these families.

This inaccurate and biased view of such families has meant that the pleasure and rewards of parenting a disabled child have not been considered. It was almost as if we could not believe that parents could actually love children who looked or behaved 'abnormally', or that such children could ever be a source of joy. Although such views might be less extreme nowadays, research is still failing to give much attention to exploring the positive aspects of caring for a disabled child. It is also continuing to ignore the enormous role that feelings and emotions play in maintaining family life. Until research can look at the child as the parents do, we will never fully understand how parents manage, and what 'keeps them going'. As noted in the previous chapter, parents do not look at their child and see disability; rather they look and see their child – their son or their daughter.

This chapter will try to put the reader in the 'parent's shoes' in order to understand more clearly why most parents continue to care for their disabled child at home, and indeed positively choose to do so.

A way of life
For the parent, caring for a disabled child is an integral part of their daily life (Featherstone, 1980). Many parents felt there was nothing extraordinary about them or their child. The fact that their child was part of their lives on a day-to-day basis made any differences or difficulties, which were highly apparent to an onlooker, unremarkable.

This is not to say that soon after diagnosis, parents were unaware of the enormous extra efforts they were having to make in order to care for their child. However, it seemed that over time the process of meeting the child's needs was assimilated into family life. This might in part be due to parents becoming more skilled at meeting those various needs. However, caring for a child on a daily basis also means that it can become, as one parent put it, 'just a way of life'. This was revealed both in the general approach they had taken to bringing up their child, and also in more specific ways, such as how they perceived having to take extra time to teach the child new skills. This parent is describing the way that bringing up a blind child changed from being a conscious effort to an unquestioned part of life.

> It's something I don't notice any more. When she was very young you were always striving to keep her stimulated, to stay ahead of her. You thought 'I've got to do something different now – to keep her stimulated, to keep her going'. Now it's just a way of life.
> (Thompson)

Similarly, parents of children with learning difficulties found that teaching the child any new skill took time and perseverance, and they could not assume that the child would automatically learn anything. As a result very deliberate efforts have to be made. However, with time, teaching the child and adopting particular approaches to teaching occur unconsciously.

> It's just a matter of keeping on. I don't even do it consciously. I just sort of sit and do things with her.
> (Whiting)

No choice
It would be wrong to say that the parents never spoke about giving up or wishing someone else could take responsibility for the child. Often these feelings were discussed in relation to a particular crisis event. In such circumstances some parents felt that the only reason they carried on was because there was no option, and taking any other course of action would be futile.

> M   You can get a week and it's been a bit grotty all week, and you've had a couple of nasty 'do's' with him and you've got a lot of other things on. At those times you just think 'God ... this is horrible and I don't like it'.
> I   And what do you do when you feel like that?
> M   What can you do? You carry on, don't you? There's not an awful lot else you can do.
> (Forsyth)

> Nothing stops does it? You just carry on because they're there ... so you have to. There's nothing else to do.
> (Walker)

However, parents also spoke about there being no choice in a different way. Here they were talking at a broader level about their decision to care for the child at home, or explaining why they carried on despite the strains and difficulties they encountered. Parents felt that although, objectively, there was a choice, the emotional dimension of parenthood 'rid' them of that choice.

> I   ... why do you think you manage to care for Lisa and keep her at home?
>
> M   I think anybody would really. I've often heard my friends say 'I would never cope with that', but I'm sure they would have done, you have to really. Put in the same situation you haven't got a lot of choice really. It's either love and care for this child or give it up. And I think there aren't many that could give a child up at birth, when they've just given birth – I'm sure of that.
>
> (Reeves)

It is acknowledged that the vulnerability of a newly-born baby engenders extremely strong feelings of protectiveness in parents (Bowlby, 1951; Ainsworth, 1974; Schaffer, 1977). Questions about whether they would be able manage to look after their child did not necessarily occur to parents. The immediate needs of the child and feelings for the child over-rode concerns for the future.

> She was a baby, she was our first. To us, whether there was something wrong or not, she was still a baby. She still needed us, and so we just got on with it.
>
> (Whiting)

Motivating factors

Love and a sense of responsibility

With the love parents had for their child came the selfless giving of time, energy and effort in both physical and emotional terms. Indeed, although parents usually spoke of other factors which motivated them, underneath lay the intense love they had for their child.

> We both feel that you'd have to be a pretty callous parent not to do what we do for our child. It's only the fact that we love her so much that makes us do what we do. That's the bottom line of it, that's why you do it.
>
> (Davies)

One parent recalled seeing families going to enormous lengths to ensure the best treatment for their disabled child before her own child had developed problems. She had since endured a long battle with local authorities and health professionals about her child's diagnosis and schooling, and now compared her experiences with those of the families she had seen on television.

> I would never have dreamt of doing some of the things we've done, but at the end of the day it's your own child and you'll do it. It's like I used to watch telly and these people that sold their houses to go to America for some treatment. I thought 'Oh ... you know' ... I know now I'd do it.
> (Walker)

There was also a link between acting from love and the responsibility felt as a parent to care for the child.

> You want to do it because he's your son and you love him.
> (Forsyth)

Some parents felt that since they had decided to have a child it was their responsibility to manage to care for that child once born. One mother, speaking about all her children, said:

> I brought them here, it's not their fault they're here. So I'm here to look after them and do what I can for them.
> (Carver)

In some cases it seemed that this sense of responsibility might prevent parents from being able to share the responsibility for care with formal agencies. This parent was talking about why she would not use respite care services:

> M   I couldn't put him in a home. I know I couldn't.
> I   Why's that?
> M   The fact that he's Ian and he's mine. The fact that he's me son. It's as simple as that.
> (Currey)

This sense of responsibility is open to abuse or exploitation by service providers. If parents feel they should be entirely responsible for the care of their child they are unlikely to seek formal support. While this may suit the over-stretched budgets of local authorities, the outcome may, in the long term, be detrimental to both parent and child. Linked to this is our finding that parents viewed themselves as parents and not as carers, and even found applying the term 'carer' to their situation offensive.

> I   How would you feel about being talked about as a carer?
> M   I totally object. I am a mother of an invalid child who cares for that child. I would still be a carer if he was not an invalid. I care for my children in all aspects. My feelings for them and everything I do for them. Doesn't any mother? Doesn't any father? I had my children voluntarily. I voluntarily look after them. I would like to be defined as a mother who is caring for a disabled child.
> (Currey)

The parents also identified differences between caring for a disabled child and other dependent groups of people. This was one parent's view.

> Most people want to care for their children anyway. It's just the very rare that can't cope. I think in some ways you're better off with children than older people. You've got that freedom with the child. You know that the child is going to maybe get better. Most of them are going to improve. But you can't say that with the older people.
> (Carver)

There were two parents, however, who reported that they had recently redefined their role. Both had older children with complex disabilities, and had found the child's age and the extent to which the child's needs went beyond what would usually be expected in a child of that age had provoked this shift in attitude. They saw themselves as parents *and* carers.

> I see myself as a carer as well as a parent. I think Lisa goes beyond the role of just 'parent'. I think basically that you're changing her bum for her at this age now and having to put nappies on her end and it is past just being 'parent'.
> (Reeves)

> I'm now doing so much more for her than you would expect for a nine year old that I do tend to regard myself more as a carer.
> (Hodder)

However, even where a parent did see herself, in part, as a carer, the notion of full responsibility still persisted.

> I think it's different if you've taken on an elderly parent which isn't something you have to do, or if your spouse has become disabled then you're obviously thrust into a situation you never anticipated. But as a parent you've committed yourself to care for your children for as long as they need it really.
> (Hodder)

Finally, and perhaps obviously, the love parents have for their children is the fundamental reason why parents continued to care for the child. We must consider, therefore, whether policy and practice with respect to families caring for a disabled child makes supporting the parent-child relationship a priority. If this relationship breaks down, then it is highly likely that the parent will no longer feel able to continue to look after the child. This is illustrated by the feelings of this parent, who identified herself both as a parent and as a carer, about the types of services that should be provided to families caring for a disabled child:

You should get more back-up with help [from the State] so that you're not doing so much of the caring and so you do more of the parenting. Because I can see that, though I hope to God it never happens to me, but I can see the point where somebody could come to resent the child because they're having to do all that [care tasks]. I think that could happen, it is a possibility. (Reeves)

Restricting the impact of the disability on the child's life

Where the child had some form of physical disability, the parents often spoke of their determination that the disability would not 'take over' their child's life. Parents were motivated to carry out daily treatment regimes day-in, day-out because such treatments prevented the disability getting a greater grip on their child's life. One family knew that the twice daily physiotherapy prevented, or at least delayed, their child having to use a wheelchair.

F   They have to be done and that's it. You can't turn round and say we'll forget about them because you just don't ...

M   You know that if one day you miss then sooner or later that one day will be a week, and then a problem is going to set in.

F   That's right, and we don't want that. We are determined to keep her out of a wheelchair. If it means the exercises are going to keep her out of a wheelchair then we'll do them. (Davies)

These parents saw the rewards of their efforts in terms of each day spent without a wheelchair as a 'victory' over the disabling condition.

Aside from the determination to overcome the disability in physical terms, parents were also anxious that the disability did not deprive the child of an enjoyable childhood. Again these feelings were expressed most by those parents whose children had physical disabilities, especially those where it was hoped that the disabling condition was transitory. Usually this determination was expressed in making sure the child continued with activities, such as playing in the park and going to the beach.

Giving the child the greatest possible chance

Many parents spoke about the drive to give their child the greatest possible chance in life, though this was clearly influenced by their expectations for their child. Differing expectations of educational achievements or of the ultimate degree of independence affected the ways parents brought up their children.

Despite differences in what they expected of their child, most parents felt that their aspirations were not always supported by services. They believed that it was up to them to provide as many opportunities as possible to ensure that their child would have the greatest chance in life. Furthermore, it helped parents to ease their conscience when they knew that they had tried their best for the child.

> I want her to have the best. I want her to develop to her full potential. I don't want to feel that I haven't tried to help her. (Whiting)

One parent spoke of her decision to embark on a financially costly and time-consuming treatment programme.

> Nobody was saying do this with her or do that. There was nothing for us to do. So that's why we decided we'd got to do something. If it doesn't work that's fine, but at least we'd tried. (Nicholson)

This parent later spoke about how she and her husband felt they had to 'try everything' just in case it was beneficial for the child. In those cases where the prognosis was uncertain and no clear treatment or teaching programmes were in place, some parents felt frustrated or inadequate, and that they were not 'doing enough'.

Maximising a child's chance in life also meant preparing the child for the future and, in particular, making certain that the child would achieve as much independence as possible. This seemed to be especially important to parents of children with learning difficulties and to the parent whose child was blind. One parent whose child had Down's syndrome spoke about it in this way.

> It's mainly just determination. It's a drive to see her get the best out of life as she possibly can. I don't want her to fall into the gap where she's just labelled as handicapped – it's a horrible word. But I don't want her to fall into that sort of gap. I want her to be as normal as possible. (Whiting)

Ensuring the child's happiness
Finally, parents were motivated by the desire to make their child happy. This was something that all parents were able to do and it clearly gave them a lot of pleasure.

> It's unbelievable, the silly things which we do, but we don't mind because it brings Angela on, it gets her laughing, she enjoys it. (Abbott)

Seeing their child happy also served to renew parents' attempts to care for their child in the best way possible.

> As soon as you see her smile you know everything that you felt you were going to give up all just goes out the window. As soon as she smiles you know she's happy.
> (Nicholson)

Rewards and pleasures

There are many rewards and pleasures associated with bringing up a disabled child, and these played a significant role in enabling parents to continue to care for their child, and to regard their circumstances or situation positively. The two main sources of reward were the child's successes and achievements, and the parents finding their role satisfying and enjoyable.

Successes and achievements

As with a non-disabled child, parents took great pleasure in their child's achievements. However, because' of the disability, these achievements or signs of progress were more precious, and even small successes were a source of great joy. Sometimes it was a long-awaited sign of progress.

> Once when we were at our relative's house he just stood up. Everybody started clapping – it was the first time he got up. That was nice, everybody clapping and my dad started to congratulate me.
> (Mahmood)

At other times parents spoke of a particular incident which to parents of non-disabled children would seem unremarkable. This mother had a child who sometimes found it hard to display affection.

> I went to sports day this week and he introduced me to the other children at school and said 'This is my mummy', and I felt like crying. It's the first time he'd ever done anything like that.
> (Walker)

Where the child's achievements contradicted a doctor's prognosis, the pleasure or sense of reward was heightened. A parent with a child with cerebral palsy came to the following conclusion as she reflected on the costs and the benefits of life with her child.

> I think probably the rewards have outweighed the difficulties. Every time she does something new, comes out with a new phrase. On Friday her sister said 'Be quiet!', and she turned round and said 'Shut your face!!'. Well, I don't know where she picked that up from but it was entirely new for her and it was so

spontaneous. And even something like that can be an enormous reward. Especially when you've been told she hasn't got the intelligence to learn any speech.
(Hodder)

In other instances the pleasure came from being able to have a 'normal' life when often the child's disability prevented that. This mother described a recent family outing.

We came back and we said 'We've had a lovely day!' It wasn't anything in particular, but everything just went nicely. He wasn't any problem, he'd had a good time, he'd eaten a huge picnic. He'd had a really nice pleasurable time and he hadn't caused us any problems. It was very, very satisfying for that to have happened – you almost feel normal.
(Forsyth)

Finally, signs of progress and achievement acted as positive feed-back to all the efforts parents had made to teach the child a new skill or to keep the child in the best health possible.

Enjoying the parental role

A few parents spoke specifically about the fact that they enjoyed their role and found it a satisfying experience. This was often linked with a desire not to pursue a career or go back to work. These parents felt it was an important factor in why they were able to manage.

I think one strength that was in my favour was that I've really enjoyed motherhood, more than anything else I've done in my life, and I haven't really had a hankering to go back to work. I've really enjoyed having young children at home and bringing them up. If I'd been much more career-minded I might have found it a lot more frustrating than I have.
(Hodder)

Interestingly, these parents often spoke about caring for their child as a challenge, and something they enjoyed responding to.

She's a bright girl and she's always demanded stimulation, and I take on things like that as a challenge. It's just a challenge.
(Thompson)

... with Amanda it's a challenge. If she does learn something it's wonderful. In that way she gives a lot more pleasure than my other child.
(Whiting)

This perspective or approach to bringing up a disabled child contrasts with a parent who is unhappy in the parental role, and who might view the same caring tasks as a burden or problem. Research which has looked at the role of mothers' employment supports this interpretation. It has been shown that it is not employment *per se* which affects well-being, but whether the mother is doing what she wants to do (Bradshaw and Lawton, 1978).

Other sources of reward

Parents found the reactions of other people rewarding when they acknowledged what the parent had achieved. For one parent his unusual status as a single parent father of a disabled child meant that people were interested and he was respected for what he did.

> I have a certain social standing because of the way I have coped with bringing her up, and also I brought her up on my own. There is a certain social standing from that, which is fine, it's nice. It's nice to be rewarded for, hopefully, doing something well.
> (Thompson)

This positive reaction was seen as very supportive as well as rewarding. This parent was recalling what happened at school sport's day.

> ... and they helped him out in the sack race because he couldn't cope with that. But the amount of people that came up to me and said 'oh didn't he do well' and 'Hasn't he really come on'. And that's how other people react ... they'll support you to the full.
> (Vyner)

It should be noted that parents found wide variation in people's reactions. Experiencing negative reactions was often a great source of distress. Both the children of the parents quoted above were in mainstream schooling and their disabilities, though physical, were not readily apparent. It is likely that people find it easier to react positively to such children than to those where the impairment is deforming or the child's behaviour bizarre. In addition, both these parents were well known within their village communities. As a result the contact with other people in the village might be more personal than is found in urban and inner city areas, especially where the community had known the child since birth.

The expectation that the child would recover enabled parents to deal with the difficulties of caring for their child. In our study one child was expected to recover within two to five years. The parent constantly referred to this, and it was clearly her main source of strength.

It keeps you going. We're fortunate that Martin's going to get better – it might take anything between two to five years, but it keeps you going, the fact you know he is going to get better. (Loft)

Although recovery is, without doubt, the best outcome, the temporary nature of the child's disability might make it more difficult for the parent to adapt to this period of disability. The motivation to learn ways of managing and dealing with the care of the child is lessened because parents knows it is a transitory situation. Interestingly, Martin's mother did not speak of any pleasures or rewards. The focus was very much on the hope that her child would recover quickly and, until that time, 'making do' with no attempts to turn the situation into a positive one for parent and child.

Comment

In this chapter we have tried to gain a greater understanding of why parents choose to look after their disabled child. It should be remembered that the parents in our study were all still looking after their disabled child. It may be that if the feelings and motivations we have described become exhausted, or are taken over by the negative consequences of the child's impairment, then parents will no longer feel able to cope.

We should also bear in mind that these were parents of young children, all of whom had developed problems less than eight years previously, and often relatively recently. They were still children, possessing the endearing attributes of a child, and there were signs, however small, of growth and progress. In the parents of two of the older children, both of whom had complex disabilities, there was a glimpse of the way parents' attitudes to their role may change. These parents spoke of feeling recently that they were carers of the child as well as parents. For these reasons, we believe that if parents of disabled adolescents or young disabled adults were interviewed, the findings would be different.

Summary
- Part of the process of adapting to having a disabled child appears to be the way in which parents come to perceive the demands of the disability and their families' lives as normal.
- Feelings of love and ultimate responsibility for the child were the fundamental reason why parents wanted to continue to care for their child. As a result parents felt there to be no choice about whether or not they looked after their child.
- The majority of parents identified themselves solely as parents and not as carers. It was felt that this had implications with respect to the degree to which parents expected services to

support them in this 'normal' role. Even parents who regarded themselves as carers simultaneously identified themselves as parents. These parents wanted services to support them in the caring role, leaving them time and space to be a parent to the child, since it was the parent-child relationship which ensured the child would be looked after at home.

- Parents of physically disabled children strove to restrict the impact of the impairment on the child's life. There was a sense that parents did not want to be 'beaten' by the disability.

- Parents' current efforts with their disabled child were regarded as an investment in the future. In particular, parents sought to maximise the child's chances of achieving some degree of independence.

- The children's achievements were very precious to parents, and sometimes a source of hope as well. These achievements renewed parents' energies and motivations.

- Parents enjoyed being parents. They found it rewarding. This was especially true of parents who had not found the disability had impeded their plans for a career.

- Where the impairment was known to be transitory, the parent responded differently to the situation and appeared to take a less constructive or positive approach than those parents whose children had a chronic disability.

Parents' coping strategies

So far we have described the resources parents draw on as they care for their child. In this chapter we turn from resources to strategies. By strategies we mean the things that parents actually do to manage the variety of stresses associated with caring for a severely disabled child. This includes practical problems, emotional distress and those difficulties that can never be solved but instead have to be 'lived with'. Strategies are not limited to actions but also include rationalisations and the way parents perceive or approach particular difficulties.

Previous research has shown that the ways parents cope with stress significantly affects their well-being, with certain strategies appearing to be more adaptive or effective than others (Frey *et al.*, 1989; Quine and Pahl, 1991; Sloper *et al.*, 1991; Miller *et al.*, 1992; Thompson *et al.*, 1992; Sloper and Turner, 1993). Despite such promising and important findings, research into parents' coping strategies is sparse and methodologically limited to the use of coping questionnaires or checklists which restrict the depth of information acquired. In this chapter we offer a more in-depth view of how parents cope from day to day. In order to illustrate the range of strategies that a particular problem might demand, we shall take the case of behaviour problems and the ways parents manage them. The discussion then moves on to describe more generally the coping strategies which parents used to deal with the broad range of stresses associated with caring for a disabled child.

Managing behaviour problems

For many parents, managing behaviour problems was one of the most difficult aspects of caring for their child, presenting the parent with a range of stresses which are often overwhelming.

> You just get bogged down in coping and you don't seem to think ahead, like plan a strategy or anything, you just get on with it.
> (Hodder)

Behavioural difficulties not only create problems which the parent has to resolve or manage but also cause considerable emotional distress or frustration. In addition, difficult behaviours are often quite intractable and parents have to find ways of 'living with', as opposed to solving, the difficulty. Although, in retrospect, parents sometimes wished they had sought some sort of support, the time when parents most often reach 'crisis point' with their child's behaviour is when they are alone and having to deal with the situation by themselves.

I   Are there times when you look back and think 'I should have rung her [health visitor] then', but you didn't?

M   Yes, but I think you get a bit like you've coped this morning, you'll cope a bit longer.

(Reeves)

In some cases parents had learnt how to pre-empt difficult behaviour. For example, the parents of children with Asperger syndrome tried to avoid upsetting the child's routine, or were sure to tell the child what would be happening during the day.

Everything's got to be calm and level and going along, and preferably the same things everyday, just nice and familiar routines. As far as you can you avoid situations where there are a lot of people around. You just avoid it. If you possibly can you work round things so that it's not going to happen.
(Forsyth)

Parents had also learnt to watch for signs of frustration or distress in order to diffuse the situation early on by distracting the child with a sweet, or even tickling.

A common strategy, often used at the suggestion of the health visitor or community nurse, was to use a period of 'time out' in which the child was left alone in a safe place for a period of time. 'Time out' served two purposes in that it gave both the parent and the child the opportunity to calm down.

I'll sit her on the sofa and say 'Don't move!' and she'll kick the sofa for five minutes and take it out like that.
(Dobson)

We have had to forcibly carry him upstairs and put him in his room, and I've sat and held the door closed because I've thought 'If I don't, I'm going to wallop him'.
(Forsyth)

Withholding treats and not rewarding or reinforcing bad behaviour were other strategies which parents used to try to modify, or improve, their child's behaviour. However, the extent to which these strategies worked was dependent to some degree on the child's intellectual abilities.

It is hard to cope with the aggression and some of the behaviour which is over the top. And because the understanding isn't

there you can't reason with him, and you can't withhold
something if he doesn't appreciate what that means.
(Reeves)

Sometimes professional advice was sought, though parents did not
always find it satisfactory. In some instances parents did not agree
with the advice that was given.

> We had problems with the educational psychologist. She wasn't
> very supportive. She was supposed to give us behavioural
> guidance and we didn't get it. She just suggested that when we
> had problems with his behaviour that we had 'time out' behind
> the sofa, which I didn't agree with. She had no other help,
> although it's part of her job. She didn't come forward with any
> other help.
> (Reeves)

Others found it hard to maintain the suggested way of managing
the child since it usually demanded a level of consistency and
perseverance which was difficult to adhere to in their daily lives.

> I've got a community nurse who gives me advice, and she says
> take the treats away and stick to it. But it is hard, and I must
> admit that I do give in quite a lot.
> (Dobson)

Seeking formal support for behaviour problems was not always
seen as a possible option. One parent had been reluctant to ask for
help because she was anxious not to be seen as a mother who
'wasn't coping'. In addition, some parents believed their particular
problem to be insoluble.

> I very rarely take him to the hospital. I just cope with him on a
> day-to-day basis. There's no point taking him up there because
> there's nothing they can do.
> (Carver)

Because the behaviour problems often seemed resistant to interven-
tion and there was rarely any sign of improvement, parents had also
developed strategies which helped them redefine this particular
source of stress. Many tried to understand the problem from their
child's perspective, and this, to some extent, moderated their
emotional reactions to the child's behaviour. In the following
excerpt the mother is describing a night-settling programme which
she had been pursuing for six months. It involved not going to the
child every time she cried.

> M   ... and an hour is a hell of a long time to listen to somebody
>   crying.
> I   Can you shut the noise out at all?

M   I make sure I leave the door open because I don't want her to think we've shut her off completely. She just feels lonely and neglected.
(Nicholson)

Finally, understanding the child's intellectual abilities was also important and enabled parents to appreciate that what might be construed as misbehaviour was actually a consequence of the child's impaired abilities.

Although she has the ability to grasp simple concepts she doesn't always seem to take the next stage. She can't build on what she's learnt so her actual comprehension remains at a fairly basic level. So although she can understand the situations she's in and what's going on around her, she can't really extrapolate from that to work out how to behave in a given situation for example.
(Hodder)

Direct efforts to cope with stresses

Problem-solving
During the interviews parents told us about the various idiosyncratic ways they had gone about solving some of the problems they faced while caring for their child. It is hard to group these various strategies any more tightly than merely categorising them as problem-solving strategies.

A common difficulty was dealing with people who stared at the child. Some parents chose to ignore such behaviour, other parents elected to explain what was wrong with the child.

Well I like to go and give people a lecture on what the aspects of autism are and how rude it is to talk about people like that. I would rather put people right than to think people are condemning you for something you're not really guilty of.
(Forsyth)

One reason for these different reactions to the same stress is the individual's personality and whether they feel able to approach others. In addition, the choice of strategy might reflect how much people staring upsets the parent. The parent in the above extract admitted to finding it very upsetting whereas other parents, who tended to ignore such behaviour, were not particularly concerned by it.

Managing to fit in the housework was another problem often mentioned. Again, parents had approached this problem in a number of ways. Some used their disability benefits to buy in help with the ironing and housework. Others parents chose not to continually clear up after the child, and just did it once a day. Where the child demanded a lot of attention, parents waited until the child was distracted.

> ...and wrestling, when wrestling's on, on a Saturday about four o'clock, you think 'Right, quick go upstairs and get the toilet done while he's watching the television'. You know he won't come and pester you if it's on.
> (Whitton)

Parents also organised themselves and their families' lives in such a way as to make it easier to meet the child's needs. Thus in one family where the child was on a low-fat diet, all the family ate that way to save cooking two meals. Another parent made sure that she had a bottle for her child to use when he was downstairs to save her carrying him upstairs every time he wanted the toilet. If a child did not sleep well, parents shared the room with the child to save constantly getting up through the night.

Finally, some problems were solved by avoiding certain situations. For example, one parent only went shopping when someone else could look after the child. Another parent, troubled by the way her child tried to pull his hair out when he got cross, responded by cutting the child's hair very short.

Information-seeking

The parents fell into two distinct groups with respect to their needs for information about their child's condition. Some parents were satisfied with the information provided by medical staff and other parents. Other parents actively sought information about their child's condition from other sources. It could be argued that these differences in information-seeking merely reflected the amount of information accessible from the usual sources. We suggest that it goes beyond the question of availability or ease of access. It was clear that, for some parents, seeking and collecting information was an important process and was typical of the way they handled stressful or unusual situations.

> When I got the diagnosis for Richard, we didn't know what it was and the only way I can cope with anything like that is by finding out information. I spent about a week on the telephone and I 'phoned everybody in the book. Mencap, the lot. It's the only way – that's the way I cope.
> (Walker)

Aside from helping to relieve emotional distress, information-seeking had practical benefits too. Often parents found that information concerning services and the child's rights was relatively inaccessible. Those parents who actively sought information found they were in a better position to demand the level of services their child was entitled to.

> You've got to be prepared to investigate yourself though because it's not there on offer. You have to actually ask the right questions and say the right things and know the right people. (Thompson)

Not surprisingly it was the more articulate, middle-class parents who actively sought information. None of the parents from ethnic minority groups spoke of seeking or wanting more information. It will also be recalled that these parents had no access to informal information sources such as support groups. This section has shown that those parents who did seek information found it helpful for themselves and of benefit to their child. As a result, attention must be paid by service providers to the way information can be accessed, and particular attention should be paid to addressing the needs of those with literacy problems and those from ethnic minority groups.

Taking control
Some parents found it important to become involved in decisions about and provision of services. Eight parents were very actively involved and sought to have as much control as possible, while the remaining parents did not use this sort of strategy to help them deal with raising their child.

At a fundamental level, whether or not parents used this strategy depended on the extent to which they had encountered inadequate service provision. A clear example of this came from one parent who was not using 'control-taking' strategies at the first interview but, at the time of the second interview, was using them following dissatisfaction with aspects of her child's schooling.

> I   It sounds like you have a few worries about what's going to happen.
> M   That's why I want to go up [to the school] because I'm going to keep pushing. I'm not going to sit back and let them do as they please. I want to make sure that I get through to them exactly what I want.
> (Carver)

Beyond that it seems that other factors might influence whether a parent adopts this particular strategy. First, there were no parents from ethnic minorities in the control-taking group. Secondly, more middle-class families fell into the control-taking group. Linked to both these factors is the ability to articulate points of view or opinions. In addition, it may be that expectations, both for the child and with respect to service provision, differed between the two groups. Finally, access to resources, such as a car and telephone, would significantly affect the degree to which parents can become involved.

The main area in which parents sought to become closely involved was the child's schooling. This was achieved in a number of ways. First, parents kept in close contact with the school by telephone or by making visits. One parent chose to take her child to school as opposed to using the transport service for this specific purpose.

> I take her to school and collect her. But that's my option. It would be available for her to go on transport if I wanted, but I feel it's contact with the school really.
> (Reeves)

Secondly, parents articulated their concerns and demands. Although it was not always easy for parents, they spoke of having to learn to do so. The dealings parents had with service providers were not always harmonious. In describing their various experiences parents often used words such as 'battle' and 'fight' to describe their interactions with services. Being able to engage in such confrontations required a fair amount of assertiveness and knowledge about services in order to be successful.

> We've just argued and made ourselves obstreperous really. When Jenny's disability was first diagnosed and we started having dealings with professionals we noticed that they seem to assume that parents of disabled children were stroppy and bolshie. We said we don't ever want to get that reputation and we wouldn't be like that; but frankly over the years we've just had to.
> (Hodder)

Finally, parents pursued their demands in the face of opposition. This involved knowing the correct channels through which complaints should be made and, on occasion, using more flagrant tactics!

> It's also written into the statement that he [disabled child] must have a safe environment but the school gates are always open. So we've started a campaign to get those shut. We've written to the education authority, we've written to the governors and hopefully we're going to get something done. If we don't, we'll go to the papers.
> (Walker)

Planning
In order to prevent difficult situations arising, parents tried to make plans. Sometimes this was merely a case of finding out about

wheelchair access at places the family planned to visit. Usually, however, the planning concerned future events or needs. For instance, some parents had applied to a respite care scheme so that it could be accessed with the minimum of fuss if needed in the future.

> ... and when I ever do decide that I want respite care then it will just be a matter of formality rather than having to start from scratch.
> (Whiting)

In some cases, however, plans were made because past experience had shown that the parent could not fully manage certain situations. The previous summer holidays had left two parents worn out and exhausted. As a result they had planned ways to avoid a repeat occurrence well in advance. This involved setting up respite care and applying for places on play schemes.

> M   At the end of the last summer holidays I ended up on valium for a short space of time, and looking back if I'd had support from the beginning of the summer holidays that I needed I'm sure that crisis would have been averted.
> I   So what will you be doing this summer?
> M   Well, we've got three weeks when she's away two days and a night so that will be a breathing space. Then the last two weeks my husband will take some leave so he'll be around some of the time. So I think we've organised ourselves so well as we can to cope with it this time.
> (Hodder)

Finally, two parents were planning how they were going to cope when their child became heavier. One parent was at the early stage of exploring the options of moving to a bungalow or having their current home adapted. The other parent had tried to plan well in advance for the house to be adapted to meet the needs of their child who had a deteriorating condition and would need intensive care from the parents. However, the process of application and consequent negotiations with social services had caused a series of delays. Experiences of this kind illustrate how factors outside their control can effect parents' attempts to plan for their children's future needs, and even render their strategies useless. It seems more likely that this will occur when the parent is dealing with something that requires the involvement of a statutory agency.

Self-maintenance
Caring for a disabled child is extremely wearing both physically and emotionally and we wanted to find out how parents 're-charged' themselves. We have gathered these strategies together

under the title of self-maintenance. An important part of self-maintenance for some parents is being able to take a break from caring through use of respite care or other child-care facilities, and this has been discussed in a previous chapter. In this section, therefore, we shall be dealing more with the day-to-day strategies parents use which do not necessarily require some form of service provision.

Venting emotional distress

Virtually all the parents spoke of times when they had become very upset or angry. The sources of distress varied and included the child, the disability and service provision. In Chapter Three we described how parents drew on the support of their families and friends to talk about their anger and frustration. The parents also used other strategies. In some situations it seemed that being able to cry was the only solution, and although it served to release distress, the problem often remained.

> I cry, and then start again. It's the only thing to do. The crying does release all sorts of tension, it washes out of your body. You do feel better and then you just carry on. You have to – there's nothing else to do.
> (Walker)

Dealing with anger seemed more difficult. Parents often found that leaving the child for a few minutes helped them to control their anger and not direct it at the child. Parents often got most angry or upset at times when they were alone with the child and these were times of enormous loneliness. A few parents used a friend as a means of releasing emotion.

> I have to get it off my chest straightaway. I do have quite a lot of contact with people, and most days I would be seeing somebody I knew. They'd just get the lot whether they liked it or not! They've always been pretty good, they listen and that's all I need. I don't need any comeback, I don't need any advice about how to cope, I just need to get if off my chest.
> (Reeves)

However, many parents either did not want to telephone a friend or professional, or did not have anyone who they could turn to in that way. Others found they tended to bottle things up, and could not show their distress.

> I hide a lot. I can't always let go sometimes.
> (Currey)

The need to release emotional tension is unpredictable and is not something that can wait. Meeting this particular need of parents caring for a disabled child is therefore extremely problematic for service providers. It is however crucial since it is at times of extreme frustration or anger that the disabled child may be at risk of physical abuse.

Having other interests

Many parents emphasised the importance of having other interests apart from the child and his or her disability-related needs. We have already described how friends can provide the parent with a separate life. Here we shall describe the other ways parents sought to have interests beyond the child.

Five parents had either stayed in employment or had taken on a job because they felt it was important to have something else in their lives aside from the child. Having a job gave these parents another identity and they also enjoyed the change or break from caring and parenting tasks.

> I'm going out, I'm being somebody else, and I think it's important to do that.... And also when they've been little sods it's so nice to walk out the door and say 'I'm going away from it for a couple of hours'.
> (Forsyth)

One parent found going to work distracted her from dwelling on the deterioration in her child's condition.

> I think it [her job] keeps me sane. It gives me something else to think about. I think if I was at home all the time then I'd find I was thinking more about the long term with the muscular dystrophy.
> (Greenhow)

Other parents had developed leisure interests such as doing a course or pursuing a hobby.

> I   And what about time to relax?
> M   I get that in my writing really. That's where I escape to. I also belong to the local writer's circle and we meet once a fortnight. It's not even something that Mark [husband] and I do together. It's something I do on my own, and it's my little bit of space really.
> (Hodder)

There were, however, some parents who did not have any interests or activities. Typically, these parents had very young children and were looking forward to the time when the children started school and their time was more their own.

> I want to go back to college. I want to do something for myself. Because even if Ian is going to need me for the rest of his life I've still got to have an outlet for myself.
> (Currey)

There were other reasons why some parents felt unable to pursue their own interests. Sometimes the child's condition was very unstable and required repeated hospitalisations, or the child required a number of physiotherapy sessions during the day. There is also an issue here about the availability of child care in order that parents can develop outside interests. For parents with partners it was considerably easier to pursue interests than it was for single parents. Interestingly, only one of the single parents in the study had a full-time job, and in that case the parent worked from home.

Self-indulgence

Many parents had particular treats which they gave themselves at the end of the day such as a bar of chocolate, cigarettes, a drink, a bath or a television programme.

> But do you know what motivates me, what keeps me going? It's at the end of the day when she's [disabled child] out of the way, if I can watch News at Ten and have a cup of tea then the day's been worth it no matter what day I've had.
> (Abbott)

Some also played sport regularly as their means of relaxation. Others relished an early night or an occasional lie-in. However, it should be noted these required someone, invariably the spouse, being available to look after the child.

For some parents the priority was to spend their free time with their partner, and this was a very important part of how they managed family life.

> One night a week I always feed the children early. Penny [sibling] is a bit too big to be rushed off to bed but I make her go and do something by herself, and I put Jenny [disabled child] to bed. Then we have a meal on our own, quite often have a bottle of wine with it and just spend some good time together at least once a week. It sounds a bit clinical scheduling it into the diary but I find I have to do that otherwise the time just gets eroded away.
> (Hodder)

Finally, it was very hard for some parents to unwind at the end of a day. This was especially true if the child did not settle well, and it was not unusual to find that other children in the family were also difficult at night.

> I suppose you never fully unwind because they're up during the night. We've not had a night's sleep since he [disabled child] was born, especially with having two other babies after that. Occasionally you might have a good day and you get them to

bed and start to calm down but that's not normal. The norm is more likely to be shouting and banging and everything else.
(Walker)

Approaches to life

Taking one day at a time
Virtually all parents spoke about the way they had come to approach life by taking one day at a time.

> I just cope the same as everybody else. There's nothing special, I don't have a little halo. It's just basically day to day.
> (Carver)

A variety of reasons were given for taking this particular approach. Often there was enough to deal with on a daily basis and it was not possible to spend time thinking about the future. Many parents also felt powerless with regard to planning their child's future. Where the child's prognosis or outcome was uncertain, worrying about the future was pointless.

> It's no good ruining a good life now for the next twenty years when we don't know for the next two what he's going to do.
> (Currey)

For other parents it was clear that to think into the future was too distressing, and their way of dealing with that was to live from day to day. Finally, one parent felt decisions about her child's future were not hers to make, believing that the child would make those decisions for herself.

> I try to think 'When the time comes, it will be her decision to make'. Ideally I'd like her to grow independent enough to live on her own or whatever; but that's a long way off and we'll deal with it when it comes.
> (Whiting)

By taking a day-to-day approach, it seemed that some parents were able to almost forget the child's needs or disability, and it was only certain events caused them to remember their child's disabilities.

> I know he's handicapped, there's no denying that. But it's just that you don't ever see him as being that. But when somebody looks at him and you see their expression you think 'Oh yeah, he's handicapped'. But apart from that you never do, you just live with him from day to day and never really think about it.
> (Whitton)

Not dwelling on difficulties
It seemed that experience had taught parents that dwelling on difficulties, whether present or in the future, was not helpful.

If you keep on about things that you've worried about they tend to enlarge in your head. We know what the problems are and now it's just a case of having to deal with them.
(Greenhow)

I don't let things register too deeply in my mind. I find I do that with quite a lot of things concerning Lisa. If I start to feel anything in the way of feeling that it's a shame, or I'm sorry for her, I stop myself immediately. I won't let myself go along those lines at all.
(Reeves)

In many instances not dwelling on difficulties demanded mental discipline.

You just get on with it. Once you come down in the morning you forget about that bit and you get onto the next bit. It's the only way to do it. There's so much that happens in a day, you can't be forever thinking 'Oh God, we've got this to come now'.
(Walker)

However, sometimes parents used other activities to distract their thoughts. This was particularly helpful if the parent was carrying out a stressful task.

I find feeding stressful. The fact that she doesn't chew, that really grinds at me while I'm feeding her because I know she loves her food. I find myself thinking that she's never going to sit down and enjoy a meal like we do. All this goes through my mind while I'm feeding her. So I do have the telly on, and I try and switch off, I just gaze at the telly so that my mind's elsewhere.
(Reeves)

Acceptance

One key to coping with the care of a disabled child is acceptance of the condition or impairment. Acceptance appears to be a continual process which can be threatened by events such as a rapid deterioration in the child's condition or slower than expected progress. To a certain degree the parents' level of acceptance was reflected in their expectations for the child. The following two extracts contrast what we believe to be differing levels of acceptance. The first parent appears to have accepted the child's disability to a greater extent than the second parent.

I don't religiously push her but if I feel she can do something and she's not doing it, then I'll try and get her to do it. But I'm willing to accept that if she can't do something, she can't do it.
(Whiting)

> I always knew he might be slow. I accepted that last year, but to
> say that he's retarded – no chance. I just do not agree with that.
> (Currey)

While making a distinction between different levels of acceptance,
we are not suggesting that one is better than the other. For some
parents *not* accepting the full extent of the disability may be one
strategy they use to deal with their emotional distress. By not
believing a doctor's prognosis, parents often have a greater sense of
hope. Indeed some children had achieved more than was predicted
because the parents had not accepted the doctor's prognosis for the
child. However, there will be instances when not accepting the
disability will, in the end, lead to bitter disappointment, often after a
period in which both parent and child may well have endured
hardships. The degree to which denial is possible may be limited by
the type of condition. One parent commented that he was glad there
was no possible cure for his child's blindness.

> I know it sounds strange, but one of the good things about
> Louise is that she's blind and there's nothing you can do about
> it. That is it. There is no chasing up false avenues, no operations.
> I've met lots of parents in that situation: they don't accept the
> blindness and the child – the things they have to go through just
> to try and retain some sight. So, in a way, we just had to accept it
> with Louise and that was it.
> (Thompson)

Where the situation is less clear cut the process of acceptance is
more difficult, especially when this means that the parents or the
doctors spent some time pursuing a diagnosis.

It is likely that the process of acceptance is affected by various
factors. In our study two parents believed that having a healthy
child after the disabled child was significant.

> Kerry's [sibling] made a load of difference. One way of putting
> it is that the child I was expecting when I was carrying Lisa
> [disabled child] died. Instead I was given Lisa who was totally
> different from what I was expecting. And I grieved for that child
> that died – that child which had existed in the imagination. But
> Kerry's filled that gap. It makes it so much easier because
> Kerry's totally filled what I missed out, having her was the most
> important thing I ever did.
> (Reeves)

As is apparent from the following extract, accepting the disability
released this parent from considerable emotional distress or guilt
about her feelings towards her disabled child.

> Obviously my feelings towards Lisa were a lot easier. Instead of
> wondering how she would have been, I can accept that I've got

her how she is. I don't need to do that any more because I've got that gap filled.
(Reeves)

Hope

Although most parents came to accept their child's disability, they also maintained some hope that their child might not always be disabled.

> I suppose you're always preparing yourself that she won't recover. But I would never give up the hope of it, I never will.
> (Davies)

For a few parents this hope was entirely rational. The parent whose child had Perthes disease knew her child would recover in a few years and two parents were awaiting the outcomes of treatments which were likely to improve or cure the disabling condition.

Other parents had different sources of hope such as improvements in treatment techniques and breakthroughs in research.

> When Alan was first diagnosed they'd only just found out what actually caused it – they hadn't known for years, they'd never known. So at least we had something to hope for and that's really what keeps us going, we are hoping that something will come along. Now they are actually saying it won't be long before they're ready to do clinical trials. Obviously it's going to take time but at least the hope is there.
> (Greenhow)

Even where there were no tangible reasons to do so, parents still held on to the hope that the child would recover or that the diagnosis was a mistake. Parents felt this hope was very important, it made them continue to try to do the best for their child.

> M   You still think 'He's not, they've made a mistake'. Very small parts of me think that.
> I   Do you think you need to have that – still not totally believing?
> M   Yes. It stops you giving up on him. It makes you push for normality ... or as close as.
> (Walker)

Comparing self to others worse off

A strategy commonly used when parents felt depressed or over-burdened was to compare their circumstances with others. It was not uncommon to hear a parent say 'I'm lucky' or 'we're fortunate that...'. Such comments often referred to something which the parent believed made looking after their child easier than it would be for other parents. Parents of physically disabled children often compared themselves with families caring for a child with learning difficulties which was perceived to cause far greater problems.

> I've got a bonus. There's a girl two doors up from me and she has a mentally handicapped little boy, and I just look at David and think 'God, you know, I couldn't cope with him'.
> (Loft)

For another parent, the reminder that 'there really is someone worse off than yourself' came when she took her child for hydrotherapy and saw children in wheelchairs.

> So we're lucky that we're not as bad as them. We've got that to be thankful for.
> (Davies)

However, parents did not only compare themselves to others in relation to the type or severity of the disability but also with regard to other factors such as living circumstances.

> But I'm quite happy with what we get from the [benefits] system. It's other people I feel sorry for. In our situation we're not living on the breadline, so anything's a bonus.
> (Loft)

Even parents in quite straightened circumstances used this strategy. This extract came from an interview with a single parent with three children, one of whom had learning difficulties, who had recently spend nine months in bed and breakfast accommodation.

> I get fed up the same as other people but I snap out of it. Because I consider myself to be better off than some people and luckier in a way as well.
> (Carver)

Summary

- When faced with a problem or difficulty parents react to it in some way. They may use a strategy which aims to deal with or manage the source of stress. Alternatively, a strategy which seeks to alleviate distressing emotions may be used. Often a number of strategies are adopted to deal with the various aspects of a particular stressor.

- The strategies used by parents depended on the stress being faced and the parents' resources, such as the availability of support and financial resources.

- The adequacy of services can affect how successfully parents manage to meet their needs and their child's needs. Strategies such as planning and self-maintenance are often dependent on the availability of support services. In addition, professional advice on coping with a specific difficulty, such as behaviour problems, are sometimes extremely difficult to implement on a consistent and regular basis.

- Self-maintenance strategies are an important aspect of coping. These strategies are not concerned with dealing with stresses related to the care of the child, but are used by parents to recover or recharge themselves from the rigours of caring for their child.

- Strategies which allow parents to approach their situation positively are important. These include taking one day at a time, comparing self to others worse off, not dwelling on difficulties and having some sense of hope.

Changes affecting parents' lives

It will be recalled that this research took a longitudinal approach and interviewed the parents on two occasions. Virtually all parents had experienced at least one significant change in the period of four to five months between our two visits. That changes had occurred in parents' lives within a relatively short period of time is, in itself, an important and noteworthy finding. However, our interest lies with the *implications* of changes rather than the changes themselves. Thus we did not want merely to report how many children had started school, or how many parents were experiencing family illness. Rather we wanted to identify the areas of the parents' lives, in relation to how they were able to care for the child, which were affected by the changes.

We found that one event could affect quite disparate aspects of a parent's life. Thus before moving on to describe how these parents' lives had changed over the period of their involvement in our study, it is important to demonstrate the degree of impact which a specific event can have on life as a whole. A case history illustrates how a specific event had impinged on one parent's life with both positive and negative effects.

Case history

At our first interview Ms Abbott had described how she wanted to return to the town where she had grown up. She felt isolated from her friends and her family, and missed the practical support they would be able to offer. As a result, Ms Abbott planned to move with her partner and very young disabled child as soon as possible.

By the time of the second interview the move had been achieved. The new housing was far more suitable for the child and there was plenty of room for her to crawl around. The mother was enjoying being close to her parents, and although she asked them to babysit only occasionally, she clearly found it very supportive to have them nearby since she could pop in when she liked. Ms Abbott had also renewed old friendships and found she was going out much more than before. As had been the pattern before moving, she and her partner shared responsibility for child care in the evenings and, where possible, during the day. These were the positive outcomes of the family's move.

Moving had, however, brought its own difficulties. The one which most preoccupied the parent was a deterioration in her relationship with her partner. As a result of the move, the partner had had to give up his place on a training scheme and was now unemployed. He had found this adjustment difficult and depressing, had taken to spending considerable periods of time out of the house and was less interested in looking after the child. This has caused conflict between them, and was threatening the earlier agreement to share responsibility equally for child care. The support and friendship the mother was finding in old friends and her parents may have led to her be less reliant on her partner and, as a result, they may have had less in common and less to share together.

Finally, the move to a different region had meant that Ms Abbott was having to sort out the various services for her child again. In her own words this had provide to be 'a lot of hassle, a real nuisance having to go through all the red tape of getting her into a special place'. The parent felt that because the child had not been able to attend a nursery for two months her development had regressed.

Changes in personal circumstances

Changes in personal circumstances which might appear relatively unrelated to the disabled child may well influence how well a parent is able or not to manage. These changes might not only be a source of stress but also present the parent with additional problems and responsibilities.

Worries about money had emerged as a new problem for three families, usually relating to the partner working shorter hours due to cutbacks at work. As a result, one family was considering the possibility of the mother taking on longer hours at her part-time job, though this would present its own difficulties with respect to child care. Another family had had to stop paying for private physiotherapy for their child who, as a result, was no longer receiving all the physiotherapy she needed.

Two parents reported health problems which had recently emerged. In one case it related to caring for the disabled child as the parent found she was increasingly tired from lifting her child. The second parent had health problems unrelated to the care of the child, but these were severe enough to cause concern and require referral to a hospital consultant. Improvements in health were reported by three parents. One had had a baby and was now able to return to her previous level of involvement in the care of her disabled child. The second parent's improvement in well-being came from having a break from care through the child starting school. Finally, a parent who had been suffering from stress symptoms reported feeling 'a lot better now than I did a few months back' (Dobson).

Finally, two parents found that ongoing difficulties with their ex-husbands were causing distress and were very unsettling. For one parent it was clearly a major source of stress:

In my ideal world I'd love their dad to go away and leave us alone and then us to get on and use my friends to help out. That would be my ideal situation, but it's not going to happen.
(Williams)

Development of other interests
For two parents the opportunity to develop new interests had been possible because of particular changes in the parents' circumstances. One parent had moved back to the town where she had spent her childhood years and was enjoying socialising with her old friends. In the second case, the free time that was afforded by the child starting nursery school had enabled the parent to take up a number of activities, including learning to drive, doing voluntary work and treating herself to lunch out every now and again.

I've promised myself I'm going to take driving lessons as soon as I've sent for my licence. Plus I wanted to go and do something for myself.
(Currey)

Another parent had become involved with setting up a parents' support group. The parent saw this as something very positive which would widen her interests and give her the opportunity to receive training in counselling skills. Finally, one parent had started going to an exercise class once a week, which she saw as giving her 'the opportunity to have a couple of hours doing something for myself' (Whiting).

Changes in the disabling condition
There was good and bad news when it came to changes in the disabling condition. Where the child had a potentially deteriorating condition, being able to report no change was good news, although anxiety about the child's future remained. The improvements expected by two other parents had not occurred, however. One child was still waiting for an operation and the expected signs of recovery in the other child had not emerged. Both parents were having to deal with their disappointments and adjust their expectations as to when the child might be less disabled.

Most parents had mixed news concerning changes in the child's disability. Often progress in one area of the child's life was counterbalanced with some sort of deterioration. Sometimes these improvements occurred quite spontaneously, or were the result of the natural course of the child's physical and mental development. In other situations specific events could be seen to cause improvements. The most common event related to starting or changing school. Parents noticed that not only had school improved the child's abilities but also that other difficulties had been resolved, especially the problem of settling at night and sleeping without waking up.

I   What about the problem with sleeping, getting her to go to sleep?

M   That's improved with school as well. She still cries a little. Before she was crying up to an hour, an hour and a half. Now she'll cry up to about fifteen minutes and then she's fast asleep. Although her behaviour [crying] hasn't improved, but she is obviously so tired she doesn't really care in the end.
(Nicholson)

A number of parents reported an increase in behaviour problems. Sometimes certain events seemed to have precipitated these problems, particularly changing class, or returning to school after the summer holidays. For many of the parents, behaviour problems had always been the greatest source of stress and to find these problems worsening was despairing.

It's been two things going on, because there has been the improvement in her general behaviour – especially the incontinence which has completely stopped. But at the same time this destructive streak has been getting worse not better. So it's almost as if she's been working in two directions. One problem had resolved itself to be replaced by another.
(Hodder)

Finally one child's medical condition had deteriorated since our first visit, and the parent was now responsible for the administration of various medications and had learned to manage exacerbations of her child's chest problems through the use of a portable nebuliser. This had forced significant changes on the family's daily life, especially in making plans and going out.

Changes associated with the child's development
Three children had started school and a further child was now attending full-time. The parents had, with great pleasure, noticed the way the child was developing and achieving new skills – both academically and socially. In addition, they themselves had benefited. The notion that responsibility for the child was now shared was important to parents, as was enjoyment of the break from full-time child care and the freedom this afforded to develop other interests.

Now she's at school they've just taken over completely all my worries. Anything physically-wise they're completely doing

things for me, so I can sit back now. Before I had to have all responsibility for what we did with her. It's a load taken off my mind. It's a wonderful school. It's been an absolute dream come true.
(Nicholson)

Parents of children with physical impairments found their child was becoming increasingly aware of their impairments. This presented new problems for the parent. One child was reacting against the particular treatment regime that had been imposed. Growing independence and a desire to be like 'the other children' had led to conflicts which the parent was finding increasingly difficult to handle. Another child had begun to ask questions about her condition and its likely outcome which the parent found it difficult to respond to.

> Sometimes when we do the exercises she will ask something which is upsetting, which you have not got an answer for. She will say 'Why have I got arthritis?', 'How long will I have it?', 'Will it go away?', 'Why do my legs keep hurting?'.
> (Davies)

Changes in parents' understanding of the child's condition
Four parents had been exposed to particular information about their child's condition which had substantially challenged their perceptions and expectations of the child or the condition.

Two parents of children with cerebral palsy had changed their expectations for the child having heard a talk given by an adult with cerebral palsy. One parent had decided to allow her own child to have 'normal' childhood experiences even though this might involve certain risks.

> I learn more from them [adults with cerebral palsy] than I can learn from anybody, about what their childhoods were like and what they really resented from their parents. Recently I was talking to a man with cerebral palsy and he was saying 'Let her do things, if people want to do things with her, then let her do it. OK if she breaks an arm, she breaks an arm, but other children break arms, you know. Just let her be a child'.
> (Reeves)

The second parent had rethought the priorities she had for her child. Originally she had planned to take her child to the Peto Institute in Hungary with the aim of teaching her child to walk. At the second interview her priorities had changed, and she was focusing on making sure her child had the best education.

> They both said 'It doesn't matter if he can never walk as long as he gets an education'. And since then I have looked at it

completely differently, up to that point I was quite happy for
him just to learn to walk. I'm not pushing to walk now whereas
before I'd make him. Now I'm quite happy for him to just
develop his mind.
(Williams)

Fortunately this parent was extremely satisfied with her child's
schooling. If this had not been the case, the change in perspective –
from focusing on mental as opposed to physical achievements –
might have resulted in the parent facing additional problems as she
sought to improve educational provision for her child.

The two parents of the children with Asperger syndrome had both
attended a weekend workshop which had led to a deeper understanding of the condition and the child's needs. As a result both had
become extremely dissatisfied with the educational provision available to their child. One parent was extremely anxious because, as far
as she could tell, no adequate provision for her child's education
existed in her area. The family was considering sending the child to
private school although they could not afford it. In addition, the
workshop weekend had made her consider her child's future and
the problems she might encounter.

The weekend really opened my eyes to the problems when they
are older. It was quite a stopper to realise what you're up
against. I think when we'd got him in this school and he'd done
really well, I think we felt that we'd cracked it. But then
something like that comes along and it's rocked the boat and
you think it's not like that at all. All in all I find it a bit
depressing.
(Walker)

This particular example gives a clear impression of the fragile state
in which many of these families exist. It may only take a single event
to disturb the state of equilibrium the family has sought to establish.
It is possible to imagine the 'ripple effect' of this one event. The
parent's and child's well-being are likely to be affected, financial
difficulties or moving house may result, and the 'battle' with the
local education authority is resumed.

Changes in informal support

A quarter of our sample had experienced significant changes in the
availability of support from their families. In two instances there
had been an increase in the availability of child care from family
members. The parent who had moved to the same city as her own
parents, was benefiting from the practical and emotional support
they provided. Another parent had found she had to rely on the
child's father (from whom she was divorced) to look after the child

as she had to work at weekends to supplement the family's income. The parent was not particularly comfortable with this arrangement but felt the situation was, in a sense, forced on her for financial reasons.

The serious illness of a grandmother had resulted in substantially less support for two parents, and no replacement to the support provided by these grandparents had been found. In addition, the parents found themselves in a supportive role as well as having to deal with their own emotional distress.

> I was going to the clinic with her [disabled child] in the morning, over to S _____ to get his [husband's] dad in the afternoon to take him over to G _____ to visit her [grandmother] in hospital. Then I'd come home, get them [children] bathed, changed and sorted out, and them Phil [husband] was going out in the evening taking his Dad down to the hospital again. It worked out that during the week we hardly saw each other, and I felt as if I was at the end of my tether.
> (Whiting)

Changes in the use of support groups were also found. Three parents had decided not to carry on attending their support group. One parent had attended only a few times and found she 'didn't really get anything out of it'. A parent who had used a day-time support group had had to stop attending because her child could not cope with the creche that was provided. Finally, one parent felt she no longer benefited from her group.

> I'm thinking I need something different now. I've done that, been there, done that. It's not doing anything for me. I was enjoying it for a while but now I've had enough. I don't want to keep going until it gets so boring that I really dread going.
> (Carver)

This represented a substantial change in her attitude towards the support group. It suggests that needs for support and information can change, and it cannot be assumed that once a parent has joined a support group that all such needs will continue to be met.

Changes in availability of formal support

Contact with professionals
When a child starts school the availability of formal support to the parent is significantly affected. Services such as physiotherapy and speech therapy are then provided at school, and the Portage worker no longer calls. Two parents missed the contact with these people. One parent, in particular, suddenly felt very isolated, especially since it was the first time she had been at home without any children for a number of years.

> Yes, I miss it for the company, and the first few weeks I sort of felt cut off. It took me a while to get into being on my own. Like the last time Sheila [Portage worker] came, I thought 'God, I'm not going to see anybody now! Unless I go out the door, down the shop or town I'm not going to see anybody'.
> (Currey)

One parent reported an improvement in the formal support she was receiving since she had requested that her child's case be transferred from a specialist hospital to her local hospital. The consultant there had focused on both the child's needs and the parent's needs, and organised an assessment of the home adaptations that would be necessary.

> He [consultant] was really nice and he was very understanding. He said 'How are get getting on with the lifting', and I said 'Well, I'm starting to notice that I'm doing it'. He said 'I'll get somebody to come out and discuss adaptations to your house'.
> (Reeves)

Use of respite care

Six parents had experienced or initiated some change in the use of formal respite care services. Events such as invitations to special occasions and family illness had prompted two parents to explore the possibility of using respite care occasionally. Two parents had stopped using respite care. In one case the parent found she could not get along with the respite care worker and disliked her attitude towards the disability.

> She was a nice enough woman. She got on very well with the children. But it was her attitude, her belief that I shouldn't give up hope for a cure. I can't stand people who say to me that there'll be a cure. It drives me up the wall.
> (Walker)

The second parent had to discontinue using her respite care worker because the worker was only able to come on a day when the child was at school. Since the child had started school this parent had enjoyed the break this afforded her and felt less in need of a respite care worker.

Finally two parents had begun using a respite care service. One parent, after waiting three years, had just found out about her link family and initial meetings had taken place. The parent and her daughter discussed how the respite care would benefit both the child and the rest of the family:

> M   I feel if he [disabled child] goes to a link worker it'll benefit him.

I   And what difference do you think this will make to your Saturdays?

M   Oh...what's it going to be like Susan [sibling]?

S   Freedom! It sounds like we're trying to get rid of him but we're not. It's just that I sometimes want to go out shopping with my mum but I can't because of Paul [disabled child].

M   It is lovely to have him here but sometimes I think you need that little bit of freedom, and time to spend with Susan and Peter [siblings].

(Whitton)

The second parent who had started using respite care was also extremely satisfied. She felt it was of great benefit to the whole family.

It's more relaxed, and then you're quite keen to see her at six o'clock, so it's quite nice.
(Reeves)

Both parents felt they would like to use the service more. However, they did not want to become too dependent on it.

It's a help and it's something to look forward to. I think I might be frightened that you might get used to it if you got it too regularly, and then if it got chopped off it might be a disaster area. So I wouldn't want it to become that I had to rely on it.
(Reeves)

Cuts in resources

Within the relatively brief period between our two visits three parents had faced some reduction in the services provided to their child. In all cases it was clear that cuts in service provision threatened the well-being of parent and child.

One child was meant to have begun nursery school but could not because there were no resources to fund a teaching assistant. The parent was very disappointed since she felt the child would benefit from attending nursery school. Another child had recently changed school. Although extremely satisfied with the teaching and the child's general progress at the new school, this parent found the child was receiving virtually no physiotherapy.

The physical deterioration is ever so marked, it's very notice-able. She's got quite severe scoliosis which is getting much worse. Her left arm is very tight, it was beginning to come out and she was beginning to use it, but it's gone right back now. And her left leg in particular rotates right in from the hip and she can't use it at all now whereas she was making progress towards walking, with help obviously, before.
(Hodder)

The family was now considering paying privately for physio-therapy, which they could not really afford.

Finally, one parent had been threatened with the loss of her child's teaching assistant. As a result the parent had had to attend a number of meetings which she found extremely distressing. She was still waiting for the outcome. The threat of her child losing help at school had resulted in a series of extremely traumatic events as well as conflict with the child's physiotherapist who had previously been very supportive. In addition there was the worry about how the child, who was confined to a wheelchair, would manage at school.

> I don't want him to lose out. Plus it's peace of mind. I know he's well looked after and it takes a load off your mind that there's somebody there all the time.
> (Loft)

Inadequate service provision

A number of parents had encountered difficulties with services in between our two visits. As a result, in some cases the parent stopped using the service, while in others the difficulty was ongoing.

In Chapter Four we described how a child's schooling is critical to parents. Depending on parents' satisfaction, their child's school can either be a source of enormous stress or can be, as one parent put it, a 'blessing' (Williams). Often it is difficulties at school that bring parents into conflict with service providers for the first time. Three parents were looking into the schooling options for their child on our second visit.

The problem which had emerged for all of them was that, as far as they could ascertain, there was no adequate provision for their child in their area. In light of this one parent had considered moving to an area where there was a specialist school. In the event the family decided not to move, one of the major reasons being that the parent would have to change her health visitor. The health visitor had been an enormous help since the child's birth and subsequent diagnosis, and the parent was unwilling to lose such a vital source of support. Another parent who wanted her child to go to a school for physically disabled children, as opposed to one for children with learning difficulties, found that no such school existed in her area. She had come to the decision that she would have to educate her child at home unless the education authority could offer her something that was appropriate.

> The only course of action I can see is that I'm going to end up with Lisa [disabled child] at home. They've agreed to keep her

in the nursery for the short-term but the next move would be into the learning difficulties unit where they're up to age nineteen. I just can't accept that, so she'll have to come home. At the end of the day I couldn't live with the fact that she was there. I don't think I would be doing her justice.
(Reeves)

Because of her dissatisfaction with her child's schooling this parent had already reduced the hours of her part-time job. She felt that there was so much to sort out with respect to meeting her child's needs that there was no other course of action open to her.

I need more time to get things done. I'm starting things with her [disabled child] and I'm never following them up. I've approached people about technology and then it's months before I follow anything up. And it's getting to me that I'm not following things up. I feel that these are things I've got to do for myself. The school are geared up for anything like this. If she's ever going to learn I need to try and get access to these things [technology aids for communication, electric wheelchairs, etc].
(Reeves)

This parent was not an overly anxious parent who was over-involved in her child. Instead, her reactions were driven by inadequate educational provision and a clear awareness that, as a result, her child was not being given the chance to achieve her full potential.

Another parent's experience of inadequate services concerned the provision of suitable play schemes and nurseries over the summer holidays. This parent's child was extremely demanding and in previous years the parent had found it best for her and the child to use play schemes for most of the summer break. At our first visit the parent had described the plans she had made for the approaching summer vacation. When visited four months later it emerged that the family had had a very difficult summer as they had been unable to use the play schemes because of the way the child had been treated.

He went to a play scheme...I think animals at a farm would have got treated better. It was absolutely appalling. The staff, the way they treated Paul [disabled child]. They said they cared for the special needs but Paul was the only one with special needs in there and they had no idea at all about special needs. They were spitting at him, they were kicking balls at his head. I took him out. I took him out and we had him at home. It was terrible.
(Whitton)

Emerging problems with the school transport service were troubling one parent at the second interview. As the child found it very difficult to cope with changes in routine, the parent was dismayed when, in one week, there were four different escorts, some of whom clearly did not know how to handle the child's particular difficulties. In addition the taxi did not arrive at a regular time.

> It can be people who don't know him, who think he is a naughty boy that he needs a good clout. At one point we had a lady who was coming to escort him with a six-month old baby in her arms. Another person who is escorting him at the moment, I think she has some learning difficulties herself.
> (Forsyth)

The parent had complained to the authority but did not like doing so since she was reliant on the taxi service and did not want to develop a 'very bad relationship' with the taxi firm. She confessed that it was only when 'things came to a head' that she had complained and that they tried 'living with things as much as they can'. As a result this parent was tolerating what was clearly an unacceptable situation with regard to her child's transport to and from school.

Expected changes not occurring

In some cases we found that little progress had been made in overcoming particular difficulties or meeting certain needs. Parents were still waiting for their child's statement, respite care placements, an operation, and appointments with specialists. This parent was waiting for her child to have an operation.

> I wish it was all done and over. I wish it would have been done by now.
> (Baron)

Delays of this kind are extremely frustrating and leave parents feeling isolated and unsupported.

> M   It's all been a bit of a battle with Richard's education. It took us a long time to get the statement done, it took us a year and a half...twenty months to get it done.
> I   ....How do you feel about a service that's meant to be helping you but is almost being obstructive?
> M   Bitter. I feel bitter about a lot of things.
> (Walker)

Lastly, one family was still waiting for work to start on adapting their home. Numerous delays had been experienced but the parents were hoping that work would begin soon after our first visit. As it was, nothing had happened by the time of the second interview and the social services department had since raised the possibility of a contribution by the family towards the cost. The issue still remained to be resolved though it was clear the family could not afford such a payment. Alongside the frustration and strain of negotiating and waiting, the parent was having to deal with lifting and carrying an increasingly heavy child. In addition, no temporary aids were being provided to help the mother with carrying the child up and down stairs. The parent felt angry that they had been given the impression by social services that they could not begin to apply for help with home adaptations *until* the child could no longer walk.

Summary

- Most parents had experienced some change which significantly affected their lives and how they managed to care for their child. These changes included: changes in personal circumstances, development of other interests, changes in the disabling condition, changes associated with the child's development, changes in parents' understanding of the child's condition, and changes in the availability of informal and formal support.

- The impact of a single change in a parent's life can be far-reaching and can, simultaneously, have both negative and positive consequences. Even minor changes can have a substantial impact on how a parent is coping.

- A number of parents had experienced some change in the services they received. This was caused either by cut-backs in services, parental dissatisfaction with services or planned-for changes not occurring.

- Parents found unwanted or unexpected change in service provision disruptive and disturbing. It often shook their sense of being in control. The repercussions of such changes usually resulted in some period of confrontation with service providers.

Conclusion and implications

The research reported in this book differs from many studies which have looked at families caring for a disabled child. Instead of focusing on the negative aspects, we have sought to emphasise the positive. We conceived the parents' predicament differently in that we cast parents in a new role in which they were conceived as actively managing their situation rather than being passive recipients of an onslaught of stress. In taking this particular approach our interests did not lie primarily in the stresses parents unquestionably face. Rather we wanted to find out about the resources and strategies parents used to deal with the difficulties they encountered. In addition, we felt it important to gain a clearer understanding of what motivates parents to continue caring for their child, including the rewards and pleasures that parents experience. Finally, we wanted to explore how the child (as opposed to the disability) affects the ways parents are able to cope.

Key findings have been summarised at the end of each chapter. This final chapter will consider the broader issues and their implications for policy and practice. We focus on the themes of stress, support and parents as 'active agents'.

Stress
Although this study did not make the stresses experienced by parents its main focus, we nevertheless recognise the enormous difficulties and considerable distress parents often face. We found the sources of stress to be wide-ranging, and included those related to the child's care needs, emotional strains, difficulties and confrontations with service providers and negative reactions from family and members of the public. It is important to note that some of these stresses were not a necessary consequence of having a disabled child. In addition, many parents were experiencing difficulties unrelated to the disabled child. These included marital problems, bereavement and financial difficulties. We should not forget, therefore, that a parent caring for a disabled child may also be facing other stresses which, to them, may be far more problematic than those associated with the disabled child.

The majority of parents in our study appeared to have achieved some sort of equilibrium in their lives. By this we mean that the impact of stress on their lives was being balanced by three factors: how the parents were managing the stresses; positive aspects such as the relationship they had with the disabled child; and the rewards and successes they experienced as they brought up the child. However, we were also conscious that, for many parents, this state of equilibrium was extremely precarious. In particular, it was dependent on the resources upon which parents drew remaining available and reliable.

The longitudinal nature of this study enabled us to explore the ways various changes in circumstances can disrupt the degree of stability and sense of control parents feel they have over their lives. Many of the changes which adversely affected the equilibrium were both beyond parents' control and unpredictable. Sometimes they were the result of changes in the demands of the disability or a decrease in the availability of informal support. More commonly, however, they related to service provision such as the withdrawal of, or deficiencies in, services. Such changes have a two-fold impact on parents. First, parents feel they are no longer supported by formal agencies. Secondly, the changes make new demands and introduce new problems which the parent then has to deal with.

Support
Traditionally, support for parents caring for a disabled child has been conceived as having two functions. First, support should seek to meet the emotional needs of parents, and secondly, support should help parents with the care of the disabled child. The latter might include tasks such as childminding, carrying out treatments and therapies and meeting personal care needs. In addition to these particular forms of support, we would argue, our findings suggest that support for parents should be conceived in much broader terms. This would mean recognising two major points.

Support for both parent and child
First, support services for parent and child are inextricably linked. Support services for the child, such as schooling or medical treatments, are as important to the parent's sense of feeling supported as services set up to support the parent. A clear example here is the child's schooling. Dissatisfaction with schooling can leave a parent feeling at odds with service providers and isolated in his or her fight to provide the best for the child. In contrast, where parents were experiencing a high degree of involvement and interest from professionals, parents felt enormously supported.

Support services for the parent must suit or meet the child's needs as well. Parents were often reluctant to use respite care because they felt their child did not enjoy or benefit from it. Thus, however much the parent felt in need of a break, the sense of responsibility and concern for the child prevented the use of a support service for parents.

Supporting the parent-child relationship

Secondly, it is important to recognise that the fundamental function of support, whether from informal or formal sources, should be to maintain the parent-child relationship. If this relationship is supported in such a way that the parent is able to derive pleasure and satisfaction from the relationship, then it is likely that the parent will be able to continue caring for the child.

Support of the parent-child relationship can be delivered either through the parent or child-focused services. Child-focused services may include tackling sleep or behaviour problems, or ensuring that the child's impairments are minimised by appropriate treatments and therapies. Interventions of this kind will ease strain on the parent-child relationship by reducing the burden of care on the parent, thus allowing the parent to enjoy more 'quality' time with the child or, as one parent put it, to spend more time parenting and less time caring.

Support for the parent includes providing opportunities to have a break from caring for the child. Parents said that after having a break from care, through respite services or the child going to school, they looked forward to seeing their child again. Informal support can also provide parents with a rest either in terms of childminding or, more simply, by the partner taking over responsibility.

Providing adequate financial and practical resources is another key way in which a parent can be supported. Such resources can release parents from irksome care and household tasks. In addition, sufficient money can ensure that the parent is able to take the child out, and they can enjoy leisure time together. In can also pay for childminding, thus providing a break from the responsibilities of child care and time to develop other interests.

For some parents, supporting the parent-child relationship would involve making access to employment possible. Having the opportunity to go to work was a very important part of how some parents coped as it gave them social contacts and provided new interests. It is accepted that women are disadvantaged with respect to re-entering the labour market after having children. This difficulty is exacerbated for mothers of disabled children. It is essential that parents do not come to resent the child for preventing them from having a job and going out to work.

The parent also needs emotional support. Caring for a disabled child can be the source of considerable frustration and irritation.

Sometimes this is the result of dissatisfaction with services, while on other occasions it is the child who provokes such emotions. In both cases parents find themselves in a situation that is, to them, uncontrollable, and there is often no obvious vent to their emotions. Emotional support, especially that provided by informal sources, can release feelings of tension which, if left unresolved, may in the long-term threaten the well-being of both parent and child.

Vulnerability to lack of support

All the parents in the study felt unsupported in some way – either by lack of support from formal agencies or from informal sources. It is important to acknowledge that overall the level of support to parents caring for a disabled child is inadequate. Certain groups of parents may be particularly vulnerable to a lack of support, however. Specific factors appear to further predispose parents to experiencing low levels of support from formal and informal sources. Some of these factors are, in a sense, predictable and have been indicated by previous research including ethnicity, inadequate financial resources, marital status and geographical location.

In addition, we found that the nature of the child's disability influenced the extent of support. Parents of children with no specific diagnosis or with no medical needs felt unsupported by health services. If the child had a rare condition the parent did not have the opportunity to meet other parents of children with the same condition. In addition, the physical and behavioural manifestations of the disability affected the availability of informal support.

Finally, child characteristics were found to influence the extent of formal and informal support. Factors such as the child's attractiveness and their endearing qualities were seen to be important.

Parents as 'active agents' as opposed to 'passive recipients'

By defining parents as 'active agents' as opposed to 'passive recipients' we are making an important distinction. We are claiming that parents actively seek to manage the stresses and strains of caring for their disabled child. This study therefore took an innovative approach to research in this area by choosing to examine the strategies parents use to manage the problems and difficulties they encounter. We found an enormous range of strategies, and considerable creativity in the ways parents went about managing their lives and the care of their child. It is clear, therefore, that parents *do* actively seek to cope with the stresses and strains they encounter. This is not without cost, however.

In particular, parents found the resources they drew on in their efforts to cope were overtaxed. One example is the emotional support available from families and friends where, over time, parents found that family and friends were unable to meet their continuing needs. Another example is the way the parents' own health suffered. At a practical level, the drain on financial resources limited the ways parents could choose to cope.

Over-stretched resources render the parent more vulnerable to the negative impacts of stress because they are unable to cope as effectively as they might. Furthermore, because resources are under strain the advent of new stresses can significantly effect parents. As already noted, parents of disabled children often live in a fragile state of equilibrium that can be disturbed by either the onset of new difficulties or depletion in resources.

Formal support services clearly have a role to play in ensuring that parents are supported in the ways they have chosen to manage their lives. This can be achieved in two ways. First, services should support existing resources and provide resources that are not otherwise available. Secondly, services should seek to build on parents' strengths. One cannot assume that all parents cope in the same way. As a result a more individualistic approach is called for.

Coping in the future

It is important to remember that all the children in our study were young. The previous chapter gave some insight into the way that the increasing age of the child can have significant effects on the ways parents cope. For a number of reasons it would be unwise, therefore, to view these findings as applicable to parents of disabled adolescents or disabled young adults. We have been unable to explore issues such as puberty, independence and leaving home which emerge during adolescence and early adulthood. Furthermore, it is likely that parents increasingly view their role as being both parent and carer as the child grows up. Even in this study we found that parents of older children, especially those with extensive personal care needs, were experiencing changes in the way they viewed their role.

Finally, the parents in this study were all still looking after their child, and they intended to continue to do so. In a sense they could be regarded as successful copers. We could only speculate at what causes a parent to decide that he or she can no longer continue to care for the child.

Summary

- Services should seek to minimise the extent of unnecessary stress in parents' lives.
- Parents strive to achieve a degree of equilibrium in their lives in which the adverse impact of stress is balanced both by parents' attempts to manage the stress and by the parent-child

relationship. This state of equilibrium is vulnerable, in particular service provision was seen as a common cause of 'disequilibrium'.

- The principle aim of support for parents caring for a disabled child is that the parent-child relationship remains positive and rewarding. One way the parent-child relationship can be supported is through formal services for the child and for the parent.

- Special attention should be paid to groups who are vulnerable to lack of support. This includes ethnic minority groups, lone parents, parents with low incomes, parents of children with difficult temperaments or unusual appearance or behaviour.

- Parents are active and creative in the ways they manage the stresses and strains of caring for a disabled child. This demands adequate resources. Where resources are undermined or exhausted parents cope less efficiently or less successfully and are therefore more vulnerable to stress.

- If a parent is more vulnerable to stress then the disabled child's well-being and the parent-child relationship is at greater risk.

- Services should be tailored in such a way that they meet parents' resource needs, and serve to strengthen and enhance the strategies the parent has found work best for them as they care for their disabled child.

References

AINSWORTH, M.D.S. (1974) 'The development of infant-mother attachment', in CLADWELL, B.M. and RICCIUTI, H.N. (eds) *Review of Child Development Research, 3*, Chicago: University of Chicago Press.

APPLETON, P.L. and MINCHOM, P.E. (1991) 'Models of parent partnership and child development centres', *Child: care, health and development*, 17: 27–38.

BALDWIN, S.M. (1985) *The Costs of Caring*, London: Routledge and Kegan Paul.

BOSE, R. (1991) 'The effect of a family support scheme on maternal mental health of mothers caring for children with mental handicaps', *Research, Policy and Planning*, 9, 1: 2–7.

BOWLBY, J. (1951) *Maternal Care and Maternal Health*, Geneva: World Health Organisation.

BRADSHAW, J. (1980) *The Family Fund: An Initiative in Social Policy*, London: Routledge and Kegan Paul.

BRADSHAW, J. and LAWTON, D. (1978) 'Tracing the causes of stress in families with handicapped children', *British Journal of Social Work*, 8, 2: 181–192.

BRAITHWAITE, V.A. (1990) *Bound to Care*, Sydney: Allen and Unwin.

BRIDGWOOD, A. and SAVAGE, D. (1993) *General Household Survey 1991*, London: HMSO.

BROWN, A. and HEPPLE, S. (1989) *How Parents Cope: Caring for a Child who has a Handicap*, Ilford: Barnardos.

BURDEN, R.L. (1980) 'Measuring the effects of stress on the mothers of handicapped infants: must depression always follow?', *Child: care, health and development*, 6: 111–125.

BYRNE, E.A. and CUNNINGHAM, C.C. (1985) 'The effects of mentally handicapped children on families: a conceptual review', *Journal of Child Psychology and Psychiatry*, 26, 6: 847–864.

BYRNE, E.A., CUNNINGHAM, C. and SLOPER, P. (1988) *Families and Their Children with Down's Syndrome: One Feature in Common*, London: Routledge.

CAMERON, J. and STURGE-MOORE, L. (1990) *Ordinary, Everyday Families*, London: Mencap Under Fives Project.

CARVER, J. and CARVER, N. (1972) *The Family of the Retarded Child*, Syracuse, New York: Syracuse University Press.

CHETWYND, J. (1985) 'Factors contributing to stress on mothers caring for an intellectually handicapped child', *British Journal of Social Work*, 15, 295–304.

CRNIC, K.A. and BOOTH, C.L. (1991) 'Mothers' and fathers' perceptions of daily hassles of parenting across childhood', *Journal of Marriage and the Family*, 53: 1042–1050.

EISER, C. (1990) *Chronic Childhood Disease: An Introduction to Psychological Theory and Research*, Cambridge: Cambridge University Press.

FARRAN, D.C., METZGER, J. and SPARLING, J. (1986) 'Immediate and continuing adaptation in parents of handicapped children', in GALLAGHER, J.J. and VIETZE, P.M. (eds) *Families of Handicapped Persons: Research, Programs and Policy Issues*, Baltimore: Paul H. Brooks Publishing Company.

FEATHERSTONE, H. (1980) *A Difference in the Family*, New York: Basic Books.

FENNELL, G., PHILLIPSON, C. and EVERS, H. (1988) *The Sociology of Old Age*, Milton Keynes: Open University Press.

FREY, K.S. , GREENBERG, M.T. and FEWELL, R. (1989) 'Stress and coping among parents of handicapped children: a multidimensional approach', *American Journal on Mental Retardation*, 94, 3: 240–249.

GATH, A. (1985) 'Parental reactions to loss and disappointment: the diagnosis of Down's syndrome', *Developmental Medicine and Child Neurology*, 27: 392–400.

GILLEARD, C.J., GILLEARD, E., GLEDHILL, K. and WHITTICK, J. (1984) 'Caring for the elderly mentally infirm at home: a survey of the supporters', *Epidemiology and Community Health*, 38: 319–325.

GLENDINNING, C. (1983) *Unshared Care: Parents and their Disabled Children*, London: Routledge and Kegan Paul.

GLENDINNING, C. (1986) *A Single Door*, London: Allen and Unwin.

GREEN, H. (1988) *General Household Survey 1985: Informal Carers*, London: HMSO.

HEWETT, S. (with NEWSON, J. AND NEWSON, E.) (1970) *The Family and the Handicapped Child*, London: George Allen and Unwin.

HOLTER, H., HAAVIND, H. and LIPPE, A. VON DER (1982) 'Venninner' ('Female Friends'), in HOLTER, H. (ed) *Kvinner i Fellesskap (Women Together)*, Oslo: Universitetsforlaget.

JEFFORD, J. (1990) *Living with a Mentally Handicapped Child*, Norwich: Social Work Monographs.

LA GRECA, A.M. (1988) 'Children with diabetes and their families: coping and disease management', in FIELD, T.M., McCABE, P.M. and SCHNEIDERMAN, N. (eds) *Stress and Coping Across Development*, Hillsdale, New Jersey: Erlbaum.

LAZARUS, R.S. and FOLKMAN, S. (1984) 'Coping and Adaptation', in GENTRY, W.D. (ed) *Handbook of Behavioural Medicine*, New York: The Guilford Press.

LEVENTHAL, H., LEVENTHAL, E.A. and NGUYEN, T.V. (1985) 'Reactions of families to illness: theoretical models and perspectives', in TURKE, D.C. and KERNS, R.D. (eds) *Health, Illness and Families: A Life-Span Perspective*, New York: The Guilford Press.

LEVIN, E., SINCLAIR, I. and GORBACH, P. (1989) *Families, Services and Confusion in Old Age*, Aldershot: Gower.

LEWIS, J. and MEREDITH, B. (1988) *Daughters Who Care: Daughters Caring for Mothers at Home*, London: Routledge and Kegan Paul.

LONSDALE, G. (1978) 'Family life with a handicapped child', *Child: care, health and development*, 4: 99–120.

MILLER, A.C., GORDON, R.M., DANIELE, R.J. and DILLER, L. (1992) 'Stress, appraisal, and coping in mothers of disabled and non-disabled children', *Journal of Pediatric Psychology*, 17: 587–605.

MILNE, D., PITT, I. and SABIN, N. (1993) 'Evaluation of a carer support scheme for eldery people: the importance of "coping"', *British Journal of Social Work*, 23, 157–168.

MOORE, J. and GREEN, J.M. (1985) 'The contribution of voluntary organisations to the support of caring relatives', *Quarterly Journal of Social Affairs*, 1, 2.

MORONEY, R.M. (1976) *The Family and the State: Considerations for Social Policy*, London: Longman.

MOSS, P., BOLLAND, G. and FOXMAN, R. (1983) *Transition to Parenthood Project: Report to Department of Health and Social Security*, London: Policy Studies Institute.

PAHL, J.L. and QUINE, L. (1985) *Understanding and Working with Parents of Children with Special Needs*, University of Kent, Canterbury: Health Services Research Unit.

PARKER, G. (1992a) 'Counting care: numbers and types of informal carers', in TWIGG, J. (ed) *Carers: Research and Practice*, London: HMSO.

PARKER, G. (1992b) *With This Body: Caring and Disability in Marriage*, Buckingham: Open University Press.

PARKER, G. and LAWTON, D. (1994) *Different Types of Care, Different Types of Carer: Evidence from the General Household Survey*, SPRU Papers, London: HMSO.

PLESS, I.B. and ROGHMANN, K.J. (1971) 'Chronic illness and its consequences: observations based on three epidemiological surveys', *Journal of Pediatrics*, 79: 351–359.

QUINE, L. and PAHL, J. (1985) 'Examining the causes of stress in families with severely mentally handicapped children', *British Journal of Social Work*, 15: 501–517.

QUINE, L and PAHL, J. (1989) *Stress and Coping in Families Caring for a Child with Severe Mental Handicap: a Longitudinal Survey*, University of Kent, Canterbury: Institute of Social and Applied Psychology and Centre for Health Service Studies.

QUINE, L. and PAHL, J. (1991) 'Stress and coping in mothers caring for a child with severe learning difficulties: a test of Lazarus' transaction model of coping', *Journal of Community and Applied Social Psychology*, 1, 1: 57–70.

QURESHI, H. and WALKER, A. (1989) *The Caring Relationship: Elderly People and Their Families*, Basingstoke: Macmillan.

RICHARDSON, A. and RITCHIE, J. (1986) *Making the Break*, London: King's Fund Publishing Office.

SCHAFFER, R. (1977) *Mothering*, Glasgow: Fontana.

SLOPER, P., KNUSSEN, C., TURNER, S. and CUNNINGHAM, C. (1991) 'Factors related to stress and satisfaction with life in families of children with Down's syndrome', *Journal of Child Psychology and Psychiatry*, 32, 4: 655–676.

SLOPER, P. and TURNER, S. (1992) 'Service needs of families of children with severe physical disability', *Child: care, health and development*, 18, 259–282.

SLOPER, P. and TURNER, S. (1993) 'Risk and resistance factors in the adaptation of parents of children with severe physical disability', *Journal of Child Psychology and Psychiatry*, 34: 167–188.

SMYTH, M. and ROBUS, N. (1989) *The Financial Circumstances of Families with Disabled Children Living in London*, London: HMSO.

STALLARD, P. and LENTON, S. (1992) 'How satisfied are parents of pre-school children who have special needs with the services they have received? A consumer survey', *Child: care, health and development*, 18: 197–205.

THOMPSON, R.J., ZEMAN, J.L., FANURIK, D. and SIROTKIN-ROSES, M. (1992) 'The role of parent stress and coping and family functioning in parent and child adjustment to Duchenne Muscular Dystrophy', *Journal of Clinical Psychology*, 48, 1: 11–19.

TITTERTON, M. (1992) 'Managing threats to welfare: the search for a new paradigm of welfare', *Journal of Social Policy*, 21, 1: 1–23.

TIZARD, J. and GRAD, J.C. (1961) *The Mentally Handicapped and Their Families: A Social Survey*, London: Oxford University Press.

TURNBULL, A.P. (1985) 'From professional to parent', in TURNBULL, H.R. and TURNBULL, A.P. (eds) *Parents Speak Out: Then and Now*, Columbus: Merrill.

TWIGG, J. (1992) 'Carers in the service system', in TWIGG, J. (ed) *Carers: Research and Practice*, London: HMSO.

TWIGG, J. and ATKIN, K. (1993) *Carers Perceived: Policy and Practice in Informal Care*, Buckingham: Open University Press.

WALLANDER, J.L., VARNI, J.W., BABANI, L., DEHAAN, C.B., WILCOX, K.T. and BANIS, H.T. (1989) 'The social environment and the adaptation of mothers of physically handicapped children', *Journal of Pediatric Psychology*, 14, 371–387.

WIKLER, L.M. (1986) 'Periodic stresses of families of older mentally retarded children: an exploratory study', *American Journal of Mental Deficiency*, 90, 6: 703–706.

WILKIN, D. (1979) *Caring for the Mentally Handicapped Child*, London: Croom Helm.

WILLMOTT, P. (1986) *Social Networks, Informal Care and Public Policy*, London: Policy Studies Institute.

WISHART, J.G., MACLEOD, H.A. and ROWAN, C. (1993) 'Parents' evaluations of pre-school services for children with Down's syndrome in two Scottish regions', *Child: care, health and development*, 19, 1, 1–23.

ZARIT, S.H. (1989) 'Do we need another "stress and caregiving" study?', *The Gerontologist*, 29: 147–148.

Printed in the United Kingdom for HMSO
Dd297867 4/94 C10 G3397 10170

Index